Unfinished Business

Unfinished Business

*Paid Family Leave in California and the
Future of U.S. Work-Family Policy*

Ruth Milkman and Eileen Appelbaum

ILR Press
an imprint of
Cornell University Press
Ithaca and London

First published 2013 by Cornell University Press
First printing, Cornell Paperbacks, 2013

Printed in the United States of America

Library of Congress Cataloging-in-Publication Data

Milkman, Ruth, 1954– author.
   Unfinished business : paid family leave in California and the future of U.S. work-family policy / Ruth Milkman and Eileen Appelbaum.
        pages cm.
   Includes bibliographical references and index.
   ISBN 978-0-8014-5238-3 (cloth : alk. paper)
   ISBN 978-0-8014-7895-6 (pbk. : alk. paper)
   1. Parental leave—California. 2. Parental leave—United States. 3. Work and family—Government policy—California. 4. Work and family—Government policy—United States. I. Appelbaum, Eileen, 1940– author. II. Title.
   HD6065.5.U6M55   2013
   331.25'763—dc23   2013015494

Cornell University Press strives to use environmentally responsible suppliers and materials to the fullest extent possible in the publishing of its books. Such materials include vegetable-based, low-VOC inks and acid-free papers that are recycled, totally chlorine-free, or partly composed of nonwood fibers. For further information, visit our website at www.cornellpress.cornell.edu.

Cloth printing   10 9 8 7 6 5 4 3 2 1
Paperback printing   10 9 8 7 6 5 4 3 2 1

In memory of our mothers,
Beatrice Milkman and Sarah Schneider

Contents

Acknowledgments

We have been at work on this project for more than a decade. It began immediately after the California legislature passed the bill creating the nation's first paid family leave (PFL) program in the fall of 2002, when we spotted a window of opportunity—after the legislation was passed but before the program would begin operating, in mid-2004—to collect baseline data on how workers and employers were managing the kinds of family events the new PFL program would soon cover. Funding for that crucial initial stage of our research came primarily from the National Institute for Child Health and Development (NICHD). We are deeply grateful to Lynne Casper, then an NICHD program officer, who understood the uniqueness of that historical moment and guided us through the NICHD funding process, making the initial surveys of employers and workers possible on very short notice. At the Alfred P. Sloan Foundation, Kathleen Christensen supplemented the NICHD funding with a program officer's grant that supported our first round of fieldwork. The UCLA Institute for Labor and Employment also helped to fund this early stage of our work. We are also grateful to the Schumann Fund for New Jersey, and its program officer Barbara Riesman, for funding our fieldwork in that state—shortly before it became the second state to create a paid leave program, providing a valuable comparative perspective on the California case.

In 2009, we received a second round of funding for the follow-up phase of our data collection, making it possible to conduct surveys examining the impact of the PFL program on employers and workers. We thank the Ford Foundation, the Annie E. Casey Foundation, the Russell Sage Foundation, and the Rockefeller Family Fund for making this work possible. We are grateful to Anna Wadia and Helen Neuborne at Ford, Beadsie Woo at AECF, and Aixa Cintron and Eric Wanner at RSF for their generous and ongoing support for this effort. Supplementary funding also came from the California Employment Development Department, where Sandra Poole and Janet Botill provided vital support. Finally, we thank Lisa Guide at the Rockefeller Family Fund, which provided us with a dissemination grant, and the UCLA Institute for Research on Labor and Employment, which provided a planning grant for the second phase of the project.

We were fortunate to work with three different survey research centers whose skilled professional staff assisted us at many stages of the project. We thank Yuteh Cheng, Bob Lee, and Jeff Royal at the UC Berkeley Survey Research Center (which unfortunately no longer exists); Ken Gross at California Survey Research Services; and Mary Ellen Colten, Carol Cosenza, Anthony Roman, and Kirk Larsen at the Center for Survey Research at the University of Massachusetts, Boston.

Many talented graduate students helped us carry out this highly labor-intensive project over the past decade. At UCLA we were fortunate to work with Andrea Dinneen, Patricia Donze, Ana Luz Gonzalez, Marisa Gerstein Pineau, Daisy Rooks, Claudia Solari, and Anita Yuan; Rhokeun Park at Rutgers University; and finally, at the CUNY Graduate Center, David Frank, Erin Michaels, and especially Laura Braslow provided invaluable assistance. In addition, Karen White and Kristen Pipes at the Rutgers University Center for Women and Work provided excellent support for our fieldwork. Yadira Santoyo and other staff at the UCLA Institute for Research on Labor and Employment provided ongoing administrative support for this work. And at the Center for Economic and Policy Research John Schmitt helped us on several occasions with insightful advice about and analysis of various U.S. government data sets, and research assistant

Janelle Jones, program coordinator Kris Warner, and intern Alexandra Mitukiewicz also provided helpful assistance to our project. CEPR's Milla Sanes was extraordinarily helpful in designing the final graphs for the book.

We also benefited greatly from the expert advice of other researchers in this field. Donna Benton, Heather Boushey, Janet Currie, Paul Chung, Janet Gornick, Diane Halpern, Frank Neuhauser, Ann O'Leary, Judith Seltzer, Mark Schuster, and Jane Waldfogel were generous and wise in advising us on the research design. Equally crucial was the expertise of Jennifer Richard, a legislative aide to then California state senator Sheila Kuehl, who carried the bill that created paid family leave. We also learned a great deal from Tom Rankin, then president of the California Labor Federation, who helped get the PFL program legislation passed, and Rona Sheriff, then of the State Senate Office of Research, who played a key role in its implementation. Thanks also to Sharon Terman of the Legal Aid Society–Employment Law Center in San Francisco for her work on the content and design of figure 3.1.

Ellen Bravo, a tireless advocate for working women generally and family leave in particular, first at 9 to 5 and now at the Family Values @Work Consortium, also advised us at many crucial points. Our greatest debt is to Netsy Firestein, who directs the Labor Project for Working Families, and her entire staff. Netsy not only played a leading role in the advocacy and organizing that led to the establishment of paid family leave in California but also advised and supported us at every stage of the research that led to this book. Our heartfelt thanks to her as well as to Janet Gornick and an anonymous reviewer for Cornell University Press, all three of whom carefully read a full draft of this book and provided us with invaluable feedback.

Portions of this book previously appeared in "Paid Family Leave in California: New Research Findings," by Ruth Milkman and Eileen Appelbaum, in *The State of California Labor 2004* (University of California Press, 2004), 45–70, and in "Class Disparities, Market Fundamentalism and Work-Family Policy: Lessons from California," by Ruth Milkman, in *Gender Equality: Transforming Family Divisions of Labor*, ed. Janet C. Gornick and Marcia K. Meyers (Verso, 2009), 339–64, though much of the material has been revised.

Unfinished Business

1

INTRODUCTION

The Case for Paid Family Leave

California made history on September 23, 2002, when Governor Gray Davis signed a bill into law creating the nation's first comprehensive paid family leave (PFL) program. Although nearly every other country in the world guarantees paid leave to employed mothers (and in many cases, fathers as well) when they take time off to care for a new child, the United States is famously exceptional in its failure to do so.[1] Since 1993, the federal Family and Medical Leave Act (FMLA) has guaranteed *unpaid* job-protected leaves for new parents of up to twelve weeks. However, it makes such leaves available to only about half of the U.S. labor force, and even those who are covered often cannot afford to take unpaid leaves.[2] A handful of states (including California) have temporary disability programs that provide partial wage replacement to mothers during and immediately after pregnancy.[3] In the rest of the country, however, paid family leave is available only to workers whose employers provide it as part of a package of fringe benefits. With the exception of union members who often obtain such benefits through collective bargaining, non-college-educated workers and others in jobs with low pay and status often lack access even to paid sick days and paid vacation, and are even less likely to have employer-provided disability insurance or paid family leave. The growing numbers of freelancers, independent contractors, and other precarious workers who have no ongoing ties to a single employer also typically lack these basic benefits. As a result, millions of American workers are regularly forced to choose between economic security and providing vital care for their families. Against this background, California's 2002 PFL legislation was a major breakthrough, along with a similar measure that New Jersey passed into law in 2008.[4]

The Need for Family Leave

As family and work patterns have shifted in the United States, demand for time off from paid work to attend to family needs has increased dramatically. Several recent social trends have contributed to this growth. The most important among them are rising female labor force participation, especially among mothers; the aging of the population and the accompanying surge in demand for eldercare; and men's increased involvement (although it remains relatively modest) in parenting and other types of unpaid caregiving.

In the past, most family care was provided on an unpaid basis by wives and mothers, who typically withdrew from the labor force entirely when their children were young or when other family members needed assistance. But over the past century, female labor force participation rates, especially among mothers of young children, have increased dramatically; by 2010, women were 47 percent of the civilian labor force. Between 1975 and 2010 alone, the participation rate for mothers with children under age three almost doubled, rising from 34 percent to 61 percent. In a sharp historical reversal, mothers are now *more* likely to be in the labor force than women generally: the overall female labor force participation rate in 2010 was 59 percent (U.S. Department of Labor 2011a, 4–5, 19). Employment during pregnancy has also become the norm: in the first decade of the twenty-first century, about two-thirds of first-time mothers in the United States were employed while pregnant, up from 44 percent in the early 1960s (Laughlin 2011, 4). Although many women still leave the labor force for brief periods when they have children, they are far more likely than in the past to be continuously employed over the course of the life cycle. Most mothers in the twenty-first century, then, must find ways to balance the needs of their children with the demands of their jobs.

At the same time, many women today—as well as a growing number of men—are devoting considerable amounts of time to caring for elderly family members. In 2011, the U.S. Department of Labor's American Time Use Survey (ATUS) found that 19 percent of employed women and 15 percent of employed men were unpaid eldercare providers. Many of them were simultaneously engaged in parenting, making up what is popularly known as the "sandwich generation." Indeed, the ATUS found that 23 percent of adults who were providing eldercare in 2011 also had children under age eighteen in their households (U.S. Department of Labor 2012a). As the U.S. population has aged, demand for eldercare has steadily increased, and reduced family size means that the workload involved is distributed across a smaller number of children and other kin than in the past. In most families today, all adults are in the labor force, so that eldercare demands add to the challenges of balancing work and family.

Men's participation in these activities has increased somewhat in recent decades, although women continue to shoulder the bulk of unpaid childcare and eldercare alongside their paid work, a pattern Gornick and Meyers (2003) call "partial gender specialization." Historical data are fragmentary, but the ATUS found that in the 2007–11 period mothers spent 2.5 times as much time as fathers did providing physical childcare (such as feeding or bathing children) in households where the youngest child was under age six; for all childcare activities combined, the gender gap was nearly as stark: mothers spent 1.9 times as much time on childcare as fathers did (in all households with children under eighteen). Gender inequality in eldercare is less extreme but still substantial: women spent 1.5 times as much time as men did providing eldercare in 2011, according to the ATUS (U.S. Department of Labor 2012a).[5]

In regard to childcare, however, there is evidence of a generational shift: not only are younger men engaged in parenting to a greater extent than their fathers and grandfathers were, but many of them express a preference to become even more involved. Young men in long-term heterosexual relationships also face growing demands from their wives or partners to participate more fully in family life (Gerson 2010). Yet even when they do contribute substantially in terms of time, fathers remain far less likely than mothers to leave the labor force or change their hours of employment to accommodate childcare demands (Raley, Bianchi, and Wang 2012). In part, this reflects the constraints imposed by employers' inflexible scheduling demands and traditional gender norms, as well as the continuing resilience of those norms in the wider society. Nevertheless, the stresses of balancing work and family have increased substantially for men. A 2008 national survey found that 60 percent of employed fathers in dual-earner families reported experiencing "some" or "a lot" of "work-life conflict," almost double the 1977 level of 35 percent (Galinsky, Aumann, and Bond 2011, 18).

Taken together, these trends—increased maternal labor force participation, the aging of the population and the accompanying expansion in the need for eldercare, and increasing male involvement in caregiving—have led to rapid growth in demand for family leave in the United States in recent decades. Time off from their jobs can alleviate the pressures on workers during periods of peak family caregiving demand, like the arrival of a new child, or when serious illness strikes a family member. In addition, as a large body of research shows, the recipients of care benefit significantly when their family members have access to time off from work. One recent study found a negative effect on the frequency of well-baby visits, breastfeeding, and child immunizations among children whose mothers returned to work less than twelve weeks after childbirth, when compared to those whose mothers took longer leaves (Berger, Hill, and Waldfogel 2005; see also Human Rights Watch 2011, 45–50; Gornick and Meyers 2003, 242–45). Similarly, elderly patients who are cared for by family members have significantly shorter hospital stays and recover faster from illnesses than those who are not (Van Houtven and Norton 2004).

Access to *paid* time off is critically important in this context, especially for low-income workers who often cannot afford to take time off without some kind of wage replacement. One recent study found that parents who have access to paid sick leave or paid vacation time are five times more likely to stay home with a sick child than are those who lack such benefits. The consequences of this differential are far-reaching, since ill children recover more quickly when their parents are present (Heymann 2000, 59; see also American Academy of Pediatrics, Committee on Hospital Care 2003; Ruhm 2000; Schuster 2009). Yet paid time off is not available to many workers who need it. As Jody Heymann (2000) showed over a decade ago, it has typically been less available to women than men, despite the fact that women are still responsible for the bulk of family caregiving.[6] And it is far less available to the growing numbers of low-wage and precarious workers than to their counterparts in well-paid, stable jobs—even though the latter can more easily afford to take time off even without wage replacement. In short, gender and class inequalities are inextricably intertwined with the problem of access to family leave.

Family Leave and Social Inequality

A major source of gender inequality in the twenty-first century is the earnings penalty that women typically experience when they become mothers. Although outright gender discrimination in the labor market and job segregation by gender has by no means disappeared, it has been significantly reduced since the 1970s. Women's educational attainment and career aspirations have risen substantially, and gender-based wage disparities have narrowed, especially in entry-level jobs. Declining real wages for men—especially non-college-educated men—over this period also have helped to reduce the gender gap in pay. Yet that gap has by no means disappeared; indeed, it widens steadily over the typical female career, in a pattern of accumulating disadvantage (Valian 1998; Glass 2004). That motherhood is central to this process is suggested by evidence that even when they do not significantly reduce their hours of paid work, mothers' average earnings are significantly less than those of childless women (Waldfogel 1997; Budig and England 2001). The "motherhood penalty" partly reflects the persistently asymmetric gender division of housework and family care, but there is also evidence of direct employer discrimination against mothers, especially those in the managerial and professional ranks. By contrast, fathers in these occupational categories instead enjoy a wage premium (Correll, Benard, and Paik 2007).

However, even as gender inequality has lessened, class inequality has grown dramatically. The earnings gap between managers and professionals and other highly educated workers, on the one hand, and the growing ranks of low-wage workers, on the other, has widened steadily since the mid-1970s. Pay inequality has increased sharply not only among male workers but also *among women* (Bianchi 1995; McCall 2001). Endogamous marriage and mating patterns—the tendency for people to choose spouses and partners from backgrounds similar to their own—multiply these inequalities further (McCall 2010). Families are also more stable among the affluent, who typically marry at later ages and have lower divorce rates; at the other end of the economic spectrum a disproportionate number of families are headed by single mothers employed at low-wage jobs (DeParle 2012). And in dual-earner families, what were often in an earlier era "second incomes" earned by wives and mothers have become increasingly essential to meeting basic living costs (Warren and Tyagi 2003).

Inequality among women has also soared in regard to access to paid leave, as the U.S. Census Bureau (Laughlin 2011) has recently documented. As figure 1.1 shows, in the 1960s women's access to paid maternity leave

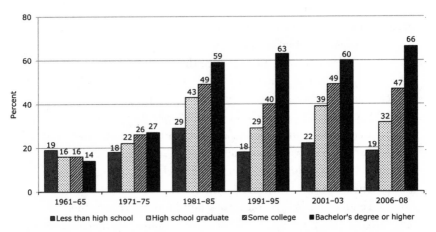

Figure 1.1. Percentage of women who received paid leave before or after their first birth, by educational attainment, selected years, 1961–65 to 2006–08. Paid leave includes all paid maternity, sick, and vacation leave, and other paid leave used before the birth and up to twelve weeks after the birth. Data from Laughlin 2011, 12.

for a first birth varied little by educational level—a reasonable proxy for social class. But that began to change in the 1970s, and the shift became increasingly apparent in the decades that followed. By the 2006–08 period, the most recent for which data are available, 66 percent of employed mothers with a bachelor's degree or more received some form of paid maternity leave before or after their first birth, whereas only 19 percent of employed women with less than a high school degree did so.

Table 1.1 exposes the main source of these disparities, namely that access to employer-provided paid time off and other fringe benefits is concentrated in the upper levels of the labor force. The data in the table are drawn from the March 2011 National Compensation Survey (NCS), a survey of employers conducted by the U.S. Department of Labor. It highlights the pattern of access to selected paid leave benefits by wage level (note that unlike figure 1.1 it includes both male and female workers). These data show that very few U.S. workers have access to paid family leave per se, although many do have access to other forms of paid time off, like paid sick leave, paid vacation, and short-term disability—which in practice are often used for wage replacement during family leaves.

TABLE 1.1 Access to selected paid leave benefits for workers in private industry and state and local government, by average wage level, March 2011 (%)

	Private industry				State and local government			
	Paid sick leave	Paid vacation	Short-term disability	Paid family leave	Paid sick leave	Paid vacation	Short-term disability	Paid family leave
All workers	63	77	38	11	89	60	23	17
Average wage in lowest 25%[a]	32	51	17	5	75	56	19	14
Second 25%	66	84	36	10	93	84	26	17
Third 25%	74	90	47	12	94	70	26	18
Highest 25%	85	89	58	19	96	36	23	18

Source: National Compensation Survey (U.S. Department of Labor 2011b).
[a] The percentile groupings are based on the average wage for each occupation surveyed in the NCS, which may include workers above and below the threshold.

The key point is that access to such benefits rises sharply with average wage levels, especially in the private sector.[7] For low-wage workers, employer-provided paid time off is extremely limited. Among those in occupations whose average wage was in the lowest 25 percent, two-thirds of private-sector workers lacked paid sick leave and nearly half had no access to paid vacation, while even greater majorities lacked access to short-term disability (83%) and paid family leave (95%). By contrast, those in occupations whose average wage was in the highest 25 percent had extensive access to various forms of paid time off.

The 2011 ATUS confirms this pattern of inequality. Based on workers' self-reports, it found that 50 percent of full-time workers whose usual weekly earnings were $540 or less (roughly the bottom 25%) had access to some form of paid leave, compared to over 80 percent of full-time workers with usual weekly earnings of $831 or more. And only 22 percent of part-time workers had access to paid leave, the ATUS found (U.S. Department of Labor 2012b).[8]

The need for financial support during leaves from work is increasingly acute for those in the bottom and middle layers of the income distribution, especially in light of the fact that real incomes for these workers have declined sharply in recent decades. Yet, as both figure 1.1 and table 1.1 show, these workers are far less likely to receive such support than are their better-paid counterparts. Many other data sources verify this pattern of class disparity. One recent survey, for example, found that two-thirds of low-income mothers, compared to slightly over a third of middle- and upper-income mothers, lose pay when they miss work because a child is sick (Kaiser Family Foundation 2003). Apart from lost income, missing work under such conditions often has other negative employment consequences— up to and including the risk of being fired, as Joan Williams (2010, chap. 2) has documented in detail (see also Williams and Boushey 2010).

Professional and managerial workers tend to have more flexible schedules (although they also work longer hours, on average) than low-wage workers, many of whom are not permitted to leave work to take a family member to a medical appointment, and indeed often may not even make personal telephone calls on "company time." Similarly, pumping breast milk at work is an option available mainly to well-paid professional women, while for lower-paid mothers it is "close to impossible," as the *New York Times* reported (Kantor 2006).[9]

The work-family problems of the majority of female workers, who labor at low wages in gender-stereotyped clerical, sales, and service "pink collar" jobs, remain relatively invisible both in scholarly literature and in public discourse, where the work-family pressures facing women in the elite professions and in high-level managerial roles receive a disproportionate share of attention (see, for example, Blair-Loy 2003; Mason and Ekman 2007; Correll, Benard, and Paik 2007; Stone 2007).[10] The media regularly feature stories about high-level female managers and professionals who have "opted out" of the workforce to devote themselves to motherhood, despite the fact that this is a minority phenomenon even within the female elite (see Williams 2010, chap. 1). A recent example that attracted extensive public attention is the 2012 article "Why Women Still Can't Have It All," by Anne-Marie Slaughter, who left her high-level post at the U.S. State Department after two years because the grueling hours it required precluded her from spending enough time with her teenage sons (Slaughter 2012).

Indeed, a well-documented class difference in regard to work-family balance involves the distinctive work scheduling patterns of low-wage workers and their more highly paid counterparts. As Jerry Jacobs and Kathleen Gerson (2004) have shown, managers and professionals (of both genders) typically must work far longer hours than they would prefer.[11] In contrast, many nonsupervisory workers seek more hours of employment than they are offered by employers, and in many cases have jobs with unpredictable, irregular, and inflexible schedules that make combining work and family extremely challenging (Lambert 2008).

Ironically, the escalating time demands on the nation's upper-tier workers emerged just when large numbers of highly educated women first gained access to elite professional and managerial jobs. Mary Blair-Loy (2003) has poignantly exposed the hegemony of the "male model" at the highest levels of the business world, where family involvement for women (as well as men) is effectively precluded by a deeply entrenched corporate culture that demands total "24/7" commitment to the firm. A less extreme version of this phenomenon pervades the elite professions and the middle management ranks. One result is that even in companies that appear to be "family friendly," available paid-time-off benefits often go underutilized (see Hochschild 1997; Glass 2004). As Blair-Loy notes, some women managers respond by "opting out," abandoning their fledgling careers (see also Stone 2007); others forgo motherhood entirely, and the rest use their abundant financial resources to hire substitute caregivers.

The expectation of extensive work hours that is so deeply embedded in managerial and professional culture conflicts directly with another set of class-specific expectations affecting affluent mothers, namely "intensive mothering" (Hays 1996). Upper-middle-class families, eager to reproduce their class position, seek to provide their children from infancy onward with a wide array of highly structured activities designed to maximize their social, emotional, and intellectual development—an effort that imposes extensive demands on mothers, as well as on the paid caregivers they employ. As Annette Lareau (2003) has documented, parenting takes a very different form in working-class communities.

Although long working hours are an especially serious problem among elite female professionals and managers, these women typically have far more extensive resources at their disposal for "work-family reconciliation" than their counterparts in clerical, service, sales, and other low-wage jobs. Well-paid professionals and managers are more able to afford the array of services—from prepared meals to paid domestic labor and childcare—on which families increasingly rely to reconcile work and family demands. And as we have already seen (in figure 1.1 and table 1.1) highly educated women and those with high earnings are far more likely than their less affluent counterparts to have access to some form of income support (through employer-provided benefits) during any leaves from work that they take to attend to family needs. When California's PFL program began operating in 2004, then, those who stood to gain the most were workers in the lower echelons of the labor market. Indeed, the new program, which was available to nearly all private-sector workers in the state, held the promise of helping to level the playing field in regard to access to paid leave.

California's Paid Family Leave Program

California's PFL program provides up to six weeks of partial wage replacement—55 percent of weekly earnings, up to a maximum benefit of $1,011 per week in 2012—for eligible workers who take time off to bond with a new child or to care for a seriously ill family member. Financed by a payroll tax, the program builds on California's long-standing State Disability Insurance (SDI) system, created in 1946 to assist workers suffering from temporary disabilities that require them to take time off from work. In the 1970s, SDI (along with its counterparts in the other U.S. jurisdictions with temporary disability insurance programs) was extended to cover pregnancy-related disability, in keeping with the policy linkage between disability and pregnancy established in that period (Vogel 1993). The PFL program extended SDI still further to cover "bonding" and "care" leaves, with benefits becoming available starting on July 1, 2004. New Jersey followed suit, implementing its Family Leave Insurance (FLI) program, generally similar to PFL in California, in mid-2009.

Like SDI, PFL is structured as an insurance program. There are no direct costs to employers: the wage replacement benefits are funded entirely by an employee-paid payroll tax that finances both SDI and PFL. (The combined tax in 2012 was 1.0% on the first $95,585 in wages.) Unlike FMLA, California's PFL program does not provide job protection, nor does it guarantee the continuation of employer-provided health insurance and other fringe benefits, although many leave-takers have these protections under FMLA or the California Family Rights Act (CFRA).

Since PFL benefits became available in mid-2004, most women employed in California's private sector who give birth to a child have been able to draw on both SDI and PFL to obtain wage replacement at 55 percent of their usual earnings for a total of sixteen to eighteen weeks. Those who take advantage of both programs typically receive SDI disability benefits for four weeks before delivery, as well as for six to eight weeks after the birth (six weeks for normal births, eight for those involving a C-section); immediately following that period they receive an additional six weeks of PFL benefits for baby bonding.

Although modest by international standards, this combined benefit is by far the most extensive publicly sponsored paid leave program for new mothers in the United States. (New Jersey's FLI program is a close second, although its maximum benefit is substantially lower—$572 per week in 2012.) California's PFL program offers wage replacement for bonding leaves not only to biological mothers but also to new fathers, domestic partners, and adoptive or foster parents, all of whom are also eligible for up to six weeks of benefits for bonding with a new child. PFL benefits are also available to workers who take time off to care for a seriously ill spouse, parent, child, or domestic partner.

The single most important characteristic of the PFL program is that, like SDI—but in sharp contrast to FMLA—its coverage is nearly universal within the private sector. FMLA covers all public-sector workers, but in the private sector it is limited to workers employed by organizations with fifty or more employees on the payroll at or within seventy-five miles of the worksite. To be eligible for FMLA, workers must also have logged 1,250 or more hours for their current employer in the year preceding the leave, and they must have worked for that employer for at least twelve months. In practice only about half the U.S. workforce, and less than one-fifth of new mothers, meet the eligibility requirements for FMLA (Ruhm 1997, 177). Moreover, many of those who are eligible simply cannot afford to take advantage of the unpaid leaves FMLA makes available.

By contrast, apart from some self-employed persons, virtually all workers in California's private sector are eligible for SDI and PFL benefits.[12] The only requirement is that claimants must have earned $300 or more in wages at a private-sector employer in the state during any quarter in the "base period" (typically five to seventeen months before filing a claim); there is no threshold for the size of the organization they work for, and they need not have worked for their current employer for any minimum period of time. Thus, under PFL and SDI paid leave is available to the growing numbers of low-wage workers, the majority of whom are female, and many of whom are precariously employed, with limited or no access to employer-sponsored benefits providing paid time off.

We have been studying the impact of PFL on California employers and workers since the bill creating the new program was signed into law in late 2002. In this book we report on the results of extensive survey research and fieldwork that we have conducted over the past decade, analyzing the ways in which the state's PFL program has benefited both workers and employers in the nation's most populous state, as well as the limitations of the program. We also explore some of the lessons that can be learned from California's pioneering PFL program—lessons that should be helpful not only to the many other states currently considering similar programs but also to the future development of family leave policies for the nation as a whole.

One key lesson involves the policy-making process itself. Historically, and especially in recent decades, legislative proposals to create new social programs have confronted formidable political challenges. For starters, U.S. employers can be relied on to vigorously oppose any efforts to introduce new forms of labor market regulation, as they have done consistently for more than a century. In recent years, concern about budget deficits and growing mistrust of government among the wider population has compounded the challenge facing public policy advocates. Many existing social programs are under political attack and others have endured severe budget cutbacks.

Yet paid family leave laws—along with related initiatives such as those mandating paid sick days for all workers—continue to enjoy widespread popular support, rooted in the steadily increasing pressures on families that struggle to balance work outside the home with caring for young children or seriously ill family members. As we document in detail in chapter 2, the deep reservoir of popular support for paid family leave made it possible to build a broad political coalition composed of women's groups, senior citizens' organizations, children's advocates, and labor unions to win passage of California's PFL bill in 2002.

In chapter 3 we provide an overview of the way the program has functioned over the past decade, reviewing the details of the program's operation and presenting data on the ways in which California workers have utilized PFL. One highlight of this chapter is the fact that male PFL claims for bonding with a new child have increased substantially and steadily over the years since the program began operating. This suggests that PFL may be helping to reduce gender inequality in the division of household and family responsibilities (see Lester 2005).

We then turn to the impact of the program on employers. Although California business groups did oppose and actively campaign against the PFL legislation, our research shows that their fears about the program turned out to have little basis in reality. As we show in chapter 4, companies have easily adapted to the implementation of PFL over the past decade, and their widely voiced concerns about abuse and of negative effects on productivity and profitability have proven to be almost entirely unwarranted. Instead, our data reveal that many employers have experienced cost *savings* as a result of PFL. The new program indirectly subsidizes employers who previously provided other forms of wage replacement during family leaves, insofar as their employees draw on the state's PFL benefits instead. Only a few employers have incurred additional costs as a result of the introduction of PFL, and even they have benefited from improved worker morale and reduced turnover.

California's PFL program also benefits workers and their families in a variety of ways, as we show in chapter 5. Not only do those who draw on PFL receive much-needed income support when they take time off to attend to family needs but recipients of care—new babies and seriously ill individuals—experience substantial health-related benefits, such as greater duration of breastfeeding and faster recovery from illness, when their family members use the program. Both men and women take longer leaves than before PFL was established (Rossin-Slater, Ruhm, and Waldfogel 2013), and they are more satisfied with the length of their leaves.

However, our research also uncovered some serious limitations of the program's effectiveness. First and most important, we found that awareness of PFL remains extremely limited among Californians. Although support for the idea of paid family leave is extensive across the state's diverse population groups, most eligible residents are not even aware that the new state program exists. Moreover, awareness is lowest among those who would benefit most from the program: Latinos, low-wage workers, younger employees, and immigrants. This has substantially limited the potential of PFL to act as a social leveler by making wage replacement for family leaves universally available, rather than being largely confined to the best-paid segments of the workforce.

Those workers who are aware of PFL, our data show, most often learn about it from their employers. And the employers who provide paid leave benefits of their own are the ones with the greatest incentive to disseminate information about the program, since, as we noted above, their expenses are reduced insofar as their employees draw on PFL instead. This dynamic tends to reproduce the longstanding inequality in access to paid leave between workers—mostly professionals and managers and other well-paid employees—who have access to employer-provided benefits and those who lack such access. Unless awareness of PFL grows among the rest of the workforce, the stark economic inequalities that characterize twenty-first century California will be reinforced more than ameliorated by the program.

We also found that some workers who *are* aware of PFL have declined to claim the benefit, even when they were eligible to use it to take time off to bond with a new child or to care for a seriously ill family member. Many of these workers reported that they feared that using PFL might have negative repercussions for them on the job, potentially reducing their chances for career advancement or even leading them to be fired. As noted earlier, PFL is structured as an insurance program, and does not include any job protection. Some workers have such protection under FMLA or CFRA, but for those who lack it and whose employers are unsympathetic to their family situations, taking advantage of PFL may indeed be risky in terms of job security. Workers' anxieties on this score have only been heightened by the high unemployment rates that California has suffered since the start of the Great Recession in 2007.

Another concern that PFL-aware workers expressed about the program, one that led some of them not to take advantage of it, is the 55 percent wage replacement level. For many workers the benefit is inadequate to meet their economic needs. For a variety of reasons, then, PFL take-up rates have been lower than expected since the program began operating in mid-2004.

At the end of this book we discuss the implications of our findings for future public policy making in the area of work-family balance, suggesting ways in which the California PFL program can be improved in the years to come. The United States has a long tradition of using states as laboratories for public policy making, in that state-level experiments often come to inform the crafting of federal legislation. With that in mind, we conclude this book with some lessons of California's experience with PFL for the rest of the country.

2

THE POLITICS OF FAMILY LEAVE, PAST AND PRESENT

In November 2011, Fox News anchor Megyn Kelly publicly chastised conservative talk-show host Mike Gallagher after he lambasted her three-month maternity leave as "a racket" on the air. Although Kelly shares Gallagher's conservative worldview and has criticized the U.S. government's "massive entitlement programs" herself on other occasions, she was outraged by his comments regarding her use of family leave. "We're populating the human race," she exclaimed. "It's not a vacation. It's hard, important work." Kelly added that the United States is "the only country that doesn't require paid maternity leave," pointing out that the FMLA provides only for unpaid leaves (Paul 2011).

As this incident suggests, attitudes about family leave do not always conform to broader political patterns. Like the underlying problem of work-family balance that it seeks to ameliorate, this is a crossover issue that elides the standard conservative denunciation of "big government." At the elite level, to be sure, political alignments on such topics are highly predictable, with most Republican elected officials and business lobbyists consistently opposing legislative proposals for family leave, while Democrats and organized labor tend to support such initiatives. But among the broader population there is a much weaker relationship between political identification and attitudes toward family leave. In that regard, Megyn Kelly's views are in no way anomalous, as can be seen in figure 2.1, which summarizes the results of a representative survey of adult Californians' attitudes toward paid leave that we conducted in the fall of 2003—a year after the bill creating the nation's first comprehensive PFL program became law.

Although there is some variation in the level of support by political orientation—as well as by gender, race and ethnicity, nativity, age, and geographical location—what is most striking is the high degree of popular consensus on this issue. That more than three-fourths of respondents who described themselves as "conservative" favored paid leave is particularly telling. These findings are consistent with those of other surveys and polls on the issue. In a 2007 nationwide poll, for example, 76 percent

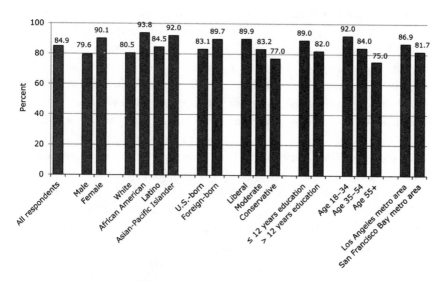

Figure 2.1. Support for paid leave among California adults, by selected characteristics, fall 2003. N = 1050. The figure shows the proportion of respondents in each subgroup who responded "favor" to the question: "Do you favor or oppose the idea of a law that guarantees that eligible workers receive a certain portion of their pay when they take family or medical leave?" For more details on the survey methodology, see Milkman and Appelbaum 2004. Data from Golden Bear Omnibus Survey, University of California Berkeley Survey Research Center.

of respondents favored expanding FMLA to guarantee paid leave (Ness 2008). Similarly, 76 percent of respondents to a 2010 national survey of registered voters indicated that they supported paid family leave laws for childbirth and family care, and 69 percent of them supported paid sick days legislation (Institute for Women's Policy Research 2010). And in a November 2012 national election night poll, 86 percent of voters nationwide said they thought it was important for Congress and the president to consider new laws like paid sick days and paid family and medical leave insurance. This poll found strong support across party lines, with 73 percent of Republicans, 87 percent of independents, and 96 percent of Democrats saying they thought this was important (National Partnership for Women and Families 2012).

This pattern of broad public support for PFL may appear paradoxical, given the political ascendancy in the late twentieth century of market fundamentalism, or "the idea that society as a whole should be subordinated to a system of self-regulated markets" (Somers and Block 2005, 261). As many commentators have noted, this perspective is especially influential in the United States, which has a long tradition of popular mistrust of the state, and indeed market fundamentalist rhetoric has contributed to the declining support for many government-sponsored social programs in recent years. Nevertheless, not only did California successfully establish its PFL program in 2002 but several other jurisdictions around the country have followed suit in the years since. In 2007, Washington State passed a paid family leave law (although funding has yet to be provided to begin operating it). The following year, New Jersey passed a law creating a family leave insurance program similar to the California PFL program, which began paying out benefits in mid-2009. In addition, paid sick days legislation was passed in three U.S. cities (Milwaukee, San Francisco, and Washington, D.C.) during the first decade of the twenty-first century, and Connecticut passed the first statewide paid sick days law in 2011. That same year, Seattle passed a paid sick days ordinance as well. Building on this momentum, in 2013 the city councils of Portland, Oregon, and New York City both passed paid sick days legislation. At this writing, campaigns for paid family leave and paid sick days legislation are under way in several other states and cities as well.[1] Could work-family legislation be an exception to the general rule that government-sponsored social programs are anathema to the majority of Americans in the twenty-first century?

The record of successful advocacy on this issue cannot be explained simply by reference to the strong public support for paid leave evident in polls and surveys like the one depicted in figure 2.1. Indeed, even a broad consensus in favor of an idea is no guarantee of its political success, especially if powerful interest groups oppose it. As we document below, the California PFL bill faced serious, organized opposition when it was proposed in 2002, led by the California Chamber of Commerce and its local affiliates. The business lobby strongly denounced the measure, claiming that PFL would impose great hardship on employers (especially small businesses), invite abuse from workers, and inflict severe economic damage on the state as a "job killer." Opponents advanced similar arguments in the other jurisdictions that passed or considered passing paid family leave and paid sick days laws in recent years.

Although the business community's countercampaign failed to prevent passage of California's PFL law, it did win some significant modifications in the configuration of the program. Whereas the original proposal included twelve weeks of paid family leave, with costs evenly split between a payroll tax on employers and one on workers, business lobbying led to elimination of the employer tax, which in turn reduced the maximum benefit to six weeks. Ultimately workers alone were required to pay the full costs of the program.[2] Pressure from business groups also resulted in an amendment providing that employers could require workers to use up to two weeks of paid vacation time before drawing on the PFL benefit (Koss 2003; Labor Project for Working Families 2003). With these modifications, the bill was passed by the California state legislature in August 2002, and signed into law by the governor a month later.

A political context where Democrats hold power may be a necessary condition of success for these types of campaigns. In California in 2002 Democrats had majorities in both houses of the legislature as well as the governorship. But this is not a sufficient condition for winning passage of laws like the one that created PFL. Two additional key elements contributed to paid leave advocates' legislative success in California and elsewhere: (a) outflanking the business lobby by organizing a wide variety of interest groups into a broad coalition in support of PFL, and (b) framing the issue with a narrative highlighting the compelling human needs addressed by paid leave, especially its positive effects on children and families. To pass California's landmark law, the advocates built a broad coalition that included women's organizations, advocates for children, senior citizens' groups, medical practitioners, organized labor, and others, capitalizing on the popular support for paid leave. The campaign leaders were also skilled at framing the issue, focusing public and media attention on the ways in which PFL would help families provide care for seriously ill loved ones and allow parents to bond with newborn babies. They also hammered home the compelling point that workers should not be forced to choose between their families and their jobs (Dorfman and Lingas 2003).

Although each of the partners in the coalition backing PFL contributed to the campaign's success, by all accounts the strong support provided by organized labor was especially critical. Labor's political influence in California was at a high point in 2002, and the California Labor Federation (the statewide AFL-CIO body) in particular had extensive lobbying experience and detailed knowledge of the legislative process. Unions not only had a long track record of winning paid leave benefits for their members through the collective bargaining process (see Gerstel and Clawson 2001) but they also had consistently supported legislation to expand such benefits for workers generally. And, crucially, the leadership of the state Federation was strongly committed to the PFL bill.

Another factor that worked in favor of PFL advocates was the fact that the proposed program was relatively simple and inexpensive to administer. The fact that it could be funded by a modest payroll tax with little or no fiscal impact immediately removed one of the standard conservative arguments from debate. In this regard it was also helpful that in California (and later in New Jersey), the bureaucratic machinery to provide temporary disability benefits was already in place, and the administration of PFL benefits could be incorporated into the existing agency's responsibilities at minimal expense. Although that particular approach is feasible only in the handful of states that already have temporary disability insurance programs, paid leave advocates have developed alternative mechanisms to administer paid leave programs in other states and nationally that similarly build on existing bureaucratic capacity—for example, by linking paid leave benefits to existing state unemployment insurance programs or to the federal Social Security system (see Workplace Flexibility 2010 and CHEFS 2010).

The political dynamics that shaped the successful campaigns for paid family leave in the states of Washington and New Jersey, and in the various jurisdictions around the country that enacted paid sick days laws in the early twenty-first century, were generally similar to those that led to PFL's successful passage in California in 2002. In each case business and employer organizations vigorously opposed the enabling legislation, yet ultimately the advocates prevailed. Passing social legislation is never easy, especially in the twenty-first century's intensely antigovernment climate. But in the nation's "blue" cities and states it can be done with a strong and well-organized coalition, including vital support from organized labor—which cannot be taken for granted, since some labor leaders, most of whom are still male, may not see this issue as a high priority—and a campaign narrative that highlights the growing pressures on workers struggling to reconcile family responsibilities with employment. Framing the issue in stark human terms, as these campaigns have demonstrated, can trump market fundamentalist rhetoric that constructs paid leave as a "job killer."

The Politics of Paid Family Leave in Historical Perspective

Employer opposition to social insurance proposals has a long history, stretching back long before the recent ascendancy of market fundamentalism. Nor is such opposition limited to the United States. As Gosta Esping-Andersen (1990, 22) pointed out in his classic comparative study of welfare capitalism, throughout the capitalist world "employers have always opposed de-commodification," defined as any service "rendered as a matter of right . . . [that allows individuals] to maintain a livelihood without reliance on the market." He classifies the United States among the "liberal" (that is, market-oriented) countries where such opposition is especially strong.[3] Indeed, for more than a century, U.S. employers have mobilized consistently to oppose not only decommodification proposals but also a variety of other basic labor regulations, ranging from minimum wage and maximum hours legislation to occupational health and safety standards.

As historians Sanford Jacoby (1997) and Jennifer Klein (2003) have shown, the result has been a nation with extremely underdeveloped state social provision alongside a "public-private welfare state" (Klein 2003) in which employer-provided health insurance and other "fringe benefits" are made available to some workers, with far more meager provision for the population as a whole.

Indeed, except in California, New Jersey, and the few other jurisdictions with temporary disability insurance programs, U.S. workers who have paid leave benefits receive them directly from employers. As a result, access to paid leave is unequally distributed across the workforce. The basic pattern is similar to that of health insurance coverage: well-paid managers and professionals are more likely than low-wage workers to have access to paid-time-off benefits; those who work for large companies are more likely to have access than those employed by small businesses or the self-employed; unionized workers are more likely to have access than their nonunion counterparts; and public-sector workers are more likely to have access than those in the private sector.

This reflects both employers' greater interest in retaining highly trained employees with firm-specific skills and the variation in bargaining leverage between union and nonunion workers, on the one hand, and between private- and public-sector workers, on the other (the latter are not only far more likely to be unionized but their employers are not seeking profit-maximization). Moreover, the costs associated with employer-provided paid family leave—unlike those for many basic labor standards such as maximum hours or paid vacation—vary enormously depending on the size of the business as well as the demographic composition of the workforce. A company whose workforce is made up primarily of women of childbearing age would have much higher costs than one with a largely male workforce, for example. The same general point applies to employer-provided health insurance, although in that case an older workforce tends to increase costs.

In contrast to health insurance coverage, however, employer-provided paid leave benefits (typically cobbled together from some combination of paid vacation, sick leave, disability insurance, and parental leave) are virtually *never* extended to workers' spouses or domestic partners—a serious limitation given the fact that men are more likely than women to have access to all types of paid-time-off benefits, even as women continue to provide the bulk of child and family caregiving. Yet, whereas a growing number of employers—faced with the huge and rapidly rising costs of providing health coverage—have lent their political support to national health insurance legislation, almost none openly support publicly sponsored paid leave programs like California's PFL—despite the fact that such programs would provide many of them with significant cost savings, as we show in chapter 4. The widely varying costs of paid family leave for different types of employers make government-sponsored social insurance, such as the California PFL program, a particularly viable approach to meeting the work-family reconciliation needs of workers, a point we discuss further in chapter 6. Nevertheless, the political reality on the ground is that the business lobby consistently opposes all decommodification legislation, whether it takes the form of social insurance or not.

The history of previous U.S. work-family legislation is instructive in this regard. Popular support for national family leave legislation gained increasing traction in the late 1970s, as more and more mothers entered the labor force. Yet even the minimalist (by international standards) FMLA became law in the face of unrelenting opposition from business interests. Fifteen years earlier, business had also opposed the Pregnancy Discrimination Act (PDA), which outlawed employment discrimination on the basis of pregnancy; with support from a coalition led by organized labor and feminist organizations it nevertheless became law in 1978 (Vogel 1993, 71). Passing national legislation on such issues became more difficult in the period of conservative ascendancy that followed the 1980 election, but advocates nevertheless began campaigning for a family and medical leave law in 1985. During the presidency of George H. W. Bush, Congress voted to approve bills similar to the 1993 FMLA twice, with significant bipartisan support, but Bush vetoed both bills. The issue was then debated in the 1992 presidential election campaign, and immediately afterward, in January 1993, Congress passed a modified version of the legislation. A month later, FMLA was signed into law by President Clinton—the very first bill he signed after taking office (Martin 2000; Bernstein 2001).

The seven-year campaign for FMLA is in many respects the prototypical case of political contestation over work-family policy in the United States. The national Chamber of Commerce and small-business groups vigorously opposed the bill, while organized labor and the women's movement led the coalition lobbying for it. As Taylor Dark (1999, 166) has documented, two key unions, the Service Employees International Union and the American Federation of State, County and Municipal Employees, both of which have large female memberships, were "key proponents of the legislation, providing financial resources, interest group coordination, and personnel for the lobbying drive." The FMLA campaign, however, was a broader coalition effort, with strong backing from the National Organization for Women and other feminist organizations that had previously worked to win passage of the PDA, along with children's advocates and others (see Bernstein 2001, chap. 5), who joined forces against the business lobby.

Cathie Jo Martin succinctly summarizes the arguments of FMLA's opponents:

> Small business predicted dire economic impacts to companies from the high costs of hiring replacement workers . . . [and] also argued that the new benefit would constrict the creation of jobs and hurt female workers by motivating employers to discriminate against women in hiring . . . and reduce the flexibility with which managers and workers could negotiate compensation packages. (Martin 2000, 221–22)

It was perfectly acceptable for companies to offer such benefits voluntarily (as many already did, especially for professional and managerial employees), but the business lobby passionately opposed any employer "mandate" in this area. As Martin rendered the business view: "Although parental and disability leaves are excellent employee benefits, Congress should not dictate benefits. Doing so is contrary to the voluntary, flexible and comprehensive benefits system that the private sector has developed." (Martin 2000, 221)

The claims that leave legislation would have negative effects on companies are largely unsupported (as we show in chapter 4 for the California PFL case), but they are an integral component of the market fundamentalism that underlies the worldview of the business lobby. That ideological orientation has proven impervious thus far to the energetic efforts of work-family advocates to articulate the "business case" for family leave—a case built around evidence that providing workers with access to leave reduces turnover, offering substantial cost savings to employers, and that such access also boosts employee morale and reduces "presenteeism," or going to work while sick (see Williams 2010, 65–71). The problem is that business opposition to family leave legislation is not rooted in evidence-based cost-benefit analysis, but rather reflects a broader animus against all types of "employer mandates," including even minimum- and living-wage laws. In the neoliberal era that began in the mid-1970s, all such proposals are routinely denounced as "job killers."

Among employers, the New Deal system of social provision has lost the limited legitimacy it once enjoyed, so that business opposition to virtually any proposal for paid leave—which is simultaneously a form of decommodification and a type of labor regulation—is a foregone conclusion. In our fieldwork we have even encountered corporate managers who, blissfully ignorant of practices in the rest of the world, go so far as to assert that the introduction of paid family leave in the United States would endanger the nation's global competitiveness. One high-level California corporate manager, in expressing her chagrin about the state's PFL law shortly after its passage, suggested that it would hurt the state economically. "That's why we moved our call center to Ireland!" she exclaimed, evidently unaware that paid leave had existed in Ireland for half a century. On the other hand, frontline and middle managers who regularly witness the challenges of work-family balance on the ground tend to be more supportive. Indeed, as Frank Dobbin has shown, in many cases human resource managers (a majority of whom are female) helped to institutionalize maternity leave in their companies in the 1970s and 1980s (Dobbin 2009, 170–75).[4]

Their market fundamentalist orientation notwithstanding, employers are able to rapidly adjust to political defeat on these issues. Thus, only a few years after the business lobby lost the battle to prevent the passage of FMLA, most companies had adapted with little difficulty to its requirements. Although there has been some concern about the extent to which FMLA's requirements are enforced (see Gerstel and Armenia 2009), a U.S. Department of Labor survey of employers conducted in 2000 found that about two-thirds (64%) of respondents found it "very easy" or "somewhat easy" to comply with FMLA rules. Moreover, 84 percent of employer respondents reported that the new law had "no noticeable effect" or a "positive effect" on their companies' productivity, while 90 percent said it had "no noticeable effect" or a "positive effect" on profitability (U.S. Department of Labor 2001). As we show in chapter 4, a decade later employers would adapt to California's PFL law with similar ease.

The History of Work-Family Legislation in California

No significant piece of federal legislation on work-family issues has been passed since 1993 when FMLA became law. At century's end, with the election of President George W. Bush, the political momentum shifted to the state and local level, beginning with California's landmark 2002 PFL bill. States have often served as incubators for innovative social programs in the past, and indeed California has played this role before. In the 1940s, the state was a leader in supporting the needs of workers for income replacement during periods of short-term disability, when they were temporarily unable to perform their normal duties on the job. The first disability insurance bills were submitted to the state legislature in 1941, although it took another five years for the bill creating what was then known as Temporary Disability Insurance (TDI) to be passed and signed into law by Governor Earl Warren, launching a program coordinated with California's unemployment compensation system.

Rhode Island had been the first state to create a TDI system, and the 1942 law establishing it there was passed with virtually no opposition. The proposal encountered opposition in California, however. As a contemporary recounted, "organized labor (state organizations of both AF of L and CIO), with the support of the Governor, was the primary proponent of the bill; employer groups and insurance companies made up the bulk of the opposition" (Osborn 1958, 54). In that regard the political alignment of forces prefigured what would emerge six decades later when PFL was debated. But there were also some striking differences between the two periods. For example, freestanding feminist organizations were not present on the political scene during the 1940s, although what Dorothy Sue Cobble calls "labor feminists" were actively engaged with social insurance issues and helped make them a priority for unions in California and elsewhere (Cobble 2004, chap. 5). The other contrast between the efforts to pass TDI in the 1940s and PFL six decades later was that whereas PFL had strong support among medical practitioners, the California Medical Association strongly opposed TDI in the 1940s. They feared TDI would be a prelude to universal health insurance, which Governor Warren and California's industrial unions were advocating at the time (U.S. Department of Labor 1952, 71; Mitchell 2002).

In 1946, once it became clear that the TDI bill had enough support in the legislature to win passage, the measure's opponents submitted an eleventh-hour amendment that would offer companies the option of purchasing private insurance plans to cover temporary disability as an alternative to participating in the state program, allowing private insurance companies to compete for the business. This amendment was incorporated into the final bill, with the additional proviso that such private disability plans would only be permitted if the benefits they offered were more extensive than those provided by the state plan (Osborn 1958, 54–55, 176).

California was not alone in creating a disability insurance program in the immediate aftermath of the war. At the federal level, the U.S. Congress passed an amendment to the Railroad Unemployment Insurance Act in 1946 providing temporary disability insurance to railroad workers. That same year Congress also passed the Knowland Amendment to the Social Security Act, which authorized states with unemployment compensation programs to use any excess funds to finance TDI benefits. Nine states had unemployment compensation programs at the time, all of which had built up large surpluses during the war period, when unemployment was virtually nonexistent.

New Jersey and New York passed TDI legislation in 1948 and 1949, respectively, both including a private insurance option similar to California's. New York's program was distinctive in that its disability insurance was coordinated with the workers' compensation system rather than with unemployment insurance. Washington State also passed a TDI law in 1949, but soon afterward opponents successfully defeated it through a referendum (Osborn 1958, 50–58). Puerto Rico and Hawaii established TDI programs much later, in 1968 and 1969, respectively (Bravo n.d., 3).

California's TDI program covered the same population as the state's existing unemployment insurance system, which meant that agricultural workers, domestic service workers, family businesses, and public sector workers were excluded from coverage. Anyone else employed by a firm with payroll over $100 in a calendar quarter was included, with no minimum firm size (in contrast, both the New York and New Jersey TDI plans excluded firms with less than four employees). The TDI benefit was initially financed by a 1 percent payroll tax on covered employees' first $3,000 in annual earnings, supplemented by surplus unemployment insurance funds (as authorized by the Knowland Amendment).

After a one-week "waiting period," any worker who had earned $300 in the "base period" (the first four of the five calendar quarters preceding a claim) was eligible for TDI benefits for up to twenty-six weeks. As a safeguard against abuse, claims had to be accompanied by certification of the disability by a physician. Benefit levels were based on a formula similar to that used for unemployment insurance, with the maximum initially set at $20 per week (Osborn 1958, 65–67; Merrick 1948, 374; U.S. Department of Labor 1952, 10). Although organized labor gradually succeeded in expanding the program in various respects—for example, extending the maximum benefit term from twenty-six to fifty-two weeks and granting coverage to agricultural workers—the $300 base-period earnings threshold remains intact to this day, for both SDI and PFL.

California's Governor Warren, an enthusiastic supporter of TDI from the outset, personally handed out the first benefit check (Bravo n.d., 13). Although it had strongly opposed the bill's enactment, five years after it began operating the state Chamber of Commerce had come to the view that the TDI program was operating smoothly, and that "malingering" (false claims of disability by workers) had not been a serious problem (U.S. Department of Labor 1952, 69). By all accounts, the program was well administered, although it did suffer occasional periods of insolvency in years when the payroll tax rates (periodically set by the legislature) were out of sync with the claims load.

The question of whether pregnancy would be a covered "disability" under TDI arose early on. "Is pregnancy to be classified as an accident or a sickness?" one commentator quipped in the 1950s (Osborn 1958, 115). In Rhode Island, where women made up 40 percent of the labor force during World War II, the disability insurance program created in 1942 had routinely compensated pregnant workers who filed disability claims; indeed, such cases made up a large proportion of the state's TDI claim load in the program's early years. After the war, however, pregnancy benefits were cut back in Rhode Island, where the state legislature introduced new restrictions on this aspect of the program, in part for financial reasons. This experience also served as a cautionary tale for the architects of TDI in California, New Jersey, and New York after the war's end; all three excluded pregnancy from coverage at the outset. The one exception in California was for pregnancies with complications that lasted beyond four weeks after delivery, which were explicitly deemed eligible for coverage (Osborn 1958, 115–17, 142–43).

Political pressure to include coverage for pregnancy under TDI programs began to mount in the 1970s, however, as maternal labor-force participation grew and a resurgent feminist movement engaged the issue. Feminists brought a new concern with gender equity to the policy arena, and most favored policies that reduced women's dependency on men and on traditional families—what Chiara Saraceno (2004) and Gosta Esping-Anderson (2009) call defamilialization. However, U.S. feminists were divided as to the optimal approach to pregnancy-related benefits. Some, not without reason, feared that creating such benefits would lead to increased discrimination against women, while others instead advocated European-style maternity leave programs for women workers. Treating pregnancy as a type of temporary disability that could be handled like other disabilities in the workplace context was a compromise, however awkward, that both camps could accept (Vogel 1993).[5]

California's TDI program was at center stage in several of the early court cases that advocates for women launched as this policy approach developed. In 1973, for example, a state court ruled that California's TDI was required to cover disability claims involving complications of ectopic pregnancies. However, in regard to the larger question of normal pregnancies the outcome was less favorable to feminist advocates. In 1974, the U.S. Supreme Court ruled in *Geduldig v. Aiello* that California's exclusion of pregnancy from coverage under TDI was legal, and did not violate the Fourteenth Amendment's guarantee of equal protection, as the plaintiffs had argued.[6] The U.S. Supreme Court issued a similar decision two years later, in a case (this time in the private sector and not directly involving California) brought by a labor union on behalf of pregnant workers who had been denied employer-provided disability benefits. In this case,

General Electric Company v. Gilbert, the court ruled that employers could legally deny sickness and accident benefits to pregnant women without violating Title VII of the 1964 Civil Rights Act, which prohibits sex discrimination in employment.

These Supreme Court decisions outraged feminists and spurred them to seek legislative action on this issue at both the state and federal levels. Their efforts soon bore fruit (Vogel 1993, chap. 5). In 1976, the California legislature amended the TDI program to include coverage for normal pregnancies for three weeks before and three weeks after delivery, a change that took effect at the beginning of 1977 (*Statutes of California* 1976, chap. 1182, 5286–87). Then in 1978 California passed legislation prohibiting pregnancy discrimination in employment and guaranteeing new mothers up to four months (eighty-eight working days) of job-protected pregnancy-related disability leave (PDL). Unlike TDI itself, which covered firms of all sizes, this new law exempted employers with less than five employees (*Statutes of California* 1978, chap. 1321, 4319–22). Later that same year the U.S. Congress passed the PDA, prohibiting discrimination against pregnant employees nationwide, effectively reversing the 1976 *Gilbert* decision. In keeping with that new federal law, in 1979 California passed legislation repealing all previous TDI provisions specific to pregnancy, effectively guaranteeing pregnant workers the same rights and benefits as workers with any other type of disability, subject to medical certification (*Statutes of California* 1979, chap. 663, 2034–36).

A decade later, another U.S. Supreme Court decision, in a case popularly referred to as *Cal Fed*, once again put California in the spotlight.[7] This 1987 case pivoted on the discrepancy between the PDA and California's job-protected pregnancy leave law. The state PDL law guaranteed leave for pregnant workers as well as reinstatement to the same or a similar job when they returned to work, regardless of whether their employers provided such job-protected leaves to workers who suffered temporary disabilities for reasons other than pregnancy. The California Federal Savings and Loan Association, the defendant in this case, denied such reinstatement to receptionist Lillian Garland when she sought to return to her job after a four-month PDL leave. The bank argued that the PDA preempted the California PDL law. Since the PDA only required that pregnancy be treated like other disabilities, and since they did not reinstate workers returning from other types of temporary disability leaves, in this case they claimed that they were not required to offer reinstatement to Garland when she returned from her pregnancy leave.

The *Cal Fed* case divided feminists once again. Those who were concerned that "special treatment" for pregnancy might increase discrimination sided with the employer, while others defended California's more generous pregnancy leave provisions and sided with the plaintiff (Garland). The Supreme Court ultimately rejected the federal preemption argument in its 1987 decision, upholding California's PDL law, which remains in effect to this day.

In 1991 the state legislature enacted the California Family Rights Act (CFRA), which took effect in 1992. Once again, as it had done with the PDA, California passed a law prefiguring one that would be enacted by the U.S. Congress soon afterward—in this case FMLA. CFRA gave private-sector employees of both genders whose employers had fifty or more workers on their payroll the right to four months of job-protected unpaid family leave to care for a newborn or adopted child, or a seriously ill family member. Less than a year later President Clinton signed the FMLA into law, with provisions that largely overlapped with CRFA. The two statutes differed slightly in regard to the scope of their coverage and also in that FMLA provided medical leaves to attend to a worker's own medical condition along with family leaves. Later in 1993, the California legislature amended CFRA to conform in most respects to FMLA, so that FMLA and CRFA leaves run concurrently and are governed by similar rules. The key exception involves pregnancy disability leaves, which for many workers in California are covered by PDL. PDL leaves typically run concurrently with FMLA (for those covered by the latter), but new mothers are entitled to another twelve weeks of job-protected leave under CFRA (in covered jobs).

California continued to be a national leader in work-family legislation in the post-FMLA era as well. In 1999, the California state legislature passed a "kin care" law requiring employers in the state who provide paid sick leave to allow their employees to use up to 50 percent of their annual allotment to care for a sick child, parent, or spouse. And finally in 2002 California passed its pioneering PFL law. Table 2.1 summarizes the highlights of work-family legislation in the state leading up to (and including) the passage of PFL. As it reveals, California has been a leader in this area for many decades, with a long history of legislation laying the groundwork for its pioneering role as the first state in the nation to create a paid family leave program.

We now turn to examine the political process that generated that historic achievement.

The Politics of California's Paid Family Leave Law

The prelude to the enactment of PFL in 2002 was a relatively obscure piece of legislation sponsored by the California Labor Federation in 1999. This was Senate Bill 656, carried by state senator Hilda Solis, who would later become U.S. secretary of labor under President Barack Obama. The bill included three components. First, it substantially increased the maximum State Disability Insurance (SDI, by now the term used in the state for what was previously called TDI) benefit level from $336 to $490 a week. This brought SDI into line with the state's workers' compensation temporary disability benefits, to which it historically had been tied (but in relation to which it had lagged since the passage of workers' compensation reform in 1993). Second, it indexed future SDI benefits to the level of those workers' compensation benefits. Finally, it required the state's Employment Development Department (EDD), the agency that administers the SDI program, to conduct a study assessing the feasibility of extending SDI to cover workers on family leave.[8]

California's SDI program already offered the longest maximum benefit duration (fifty-two weeks) among the nation's six TDI programs, and after the passage of SB 656 it provided the highest maximum weekly benefit amount as well.[9] EDD completed its feasibility study in the summer of 2000 and concluded that paid family leave could be provided within the SDI system at a very modest cost (Bernick 2000). SB 657 was only one example of how organized labor, which had been a major force behind SDI's initial creation, used its political clout over the decades to expand the program and increase the benefit level. At the turn of the twenty-first century, the California Labor Federation had especially strong political influence. Labor had long-standing ties to many Democratic elected officials, and had played a key role in helping them achieve a voting majority in both houses of the California legislature, as well as in helping to elect

TABLE 2.1. Highlights of work-family legislation in California, 1946–2002

Year	Legislation
1946	State disability program created as Temporary Disability Insurance (TDI), with pregnancy specifically excluded.
1973	TDI extended to cover disability tied to "abnormal" pregnancies (normal pregnancies remain excluded).
1976 (effective 1977)	TDI amended to cover disabilities tied to normal pregnancies for three weeks before and three weeks after delivery.
1978	Federal Pregnancy Discrimination Act prohibits discrimination against pregnant employees.
1978 (effective 1979)	State Fair Employment Practices Act amended to cover pregnancy discrimination and provide up to four months of job-protected leave for pregnancy-related disability. Small employers (with less than five employees) exempted.
1979	TDI program amended to repeal all provisions specific to pregnancy, in effect entitling disabled pregnant women to the same benefits as employees with any other type of disability. (In 1979, the maximum leave under TDI was twenty-six weeks per year; that maximum has since been increased to fifty-two weeks per year, with medical certification required.)
1991 (effective 1992)	California Family Rights Act gives private-sector employees of both genders whose employers have fifty or more workers the right to four months of job-protected family leave to care for a newborn or adopted child or a seriously ill family member.
1992	State Fair Employment and Housing Act amended to require employers with five or more employees to provide job-protected leave of up to four months for employees disabled by pregnancy.
1993	Federal Family and Medical Leave Act gives all public-sector employees, and private-sector employees of both genders whose employers have fifty or more workers, the right to twelve weeks of job-protected unpaid family or medical leave.
1999 (effective 2000)	"Kin Care" legislation requires that employers who provide paid sick leave must permit employees to use up to 50% of annual allotment to care for a sick child, parent, or spouse.
2002 (effective 2004)	SDI (formerly TDI) amended to provide paid family leave of up to six weeks per year for bonding with a newborn, adopted, or foster child or for caring for a seriously ill family member.

Democratic governor Gray Davis. Thus in August 2001, when the Federation put PFL on its legislative agenda, the political climate appeared favorable. This was a necessary—but insufficient—condition for the PFL campaign's success.

As critical to the passage of PFL as labor's early and strong support was the creation in 1999 of a Work and Family Coalition, led by the Labor Project for Working Families, an organization established in 1992 with the goal of educating unions about work-family issues and helping them win childcare and paid leave benefits in contract negotiations. The new coalition included organized labor as well as an array of advocacy groups and community organizations engaged in work-family issues, and it soon began exploring the prospects for paid family leave in the state.[10] In January 2001, the Labor Project received a planning grant from the David and Lucile Packard Foundation, providing vital resources to expand the coalition and develop the PFL campaign. This led to the formation of the Coalition for Paid Family Leave/Share the Care (hereafter the Coalition), whose founding members included the Labor Project, the California Labor Federation, Equal Rights Advocates (a women's rights litigation and advocacy organization), and the Legal Aid Society–Employment Law Center (a workplace-oriented legal services nonprofit organization). These organizations endowed the Coalition from the outset with an in-depth understanding of the complex legal and legislative issues involved in crafting a law and getting it passed, greatly facilitating the effort's ultimate success (Firestein and Dones 2007, 145; Labor Project for Working Families 2003).[11]

The Coalition began drafting the PFL legislation and contacting organizations across the state to enlist their support for the effort in early 2001, while also collecting personal stories to illustrate the need for paid leave, and searching for progressive business owners who might support PFL. At this early stage, the Coalition solicited technical advice from the National Partnership for Women and Families, the primary national advocacy group on work-family policy, and consulted policy experts in the California Senate Office of Research as well. Armed with advice from both entities, as well as the EDD's 2000 feasibility study, the Coalition commissioned a study from economists at the University of California, Berkeley, and the University of Chicago to estimate the costs and benefits of the paid family leave program for which they had drafted legislation.

That study (Dube and Kaplan 2002) found that the proposed program would cost the average employee only $2 a month—about the price of a cappuccino, as advocates often pointed out during the campaign. Employers would incur that same cost of $2 per employee per month, but would also reap significant cost savings due to reduced turnover and improved retention, the study found, while the state's taxpayers would save as well insofar as PFL benefits obviated the need for food stamps and Temporary Assistance to Needy Families.

State Senator Sheila Kuehl, at the request of the Labor Federation, agreed to be the lead author of Senate Bill 1661, which in its original draft provided twelve weeks of paid family leave, with costs evenly split between employers and workers. The proposal had a deliberately gender-egalitarian architecture, providing paid leaves to fathers as well as mothers for bonding with new babies, foster children, and adopted children; and providing caregiving leaves for both men and women to attend to seriously ill family members—spouses, domestic partners, parents, and children.[12] Because the proposed program took the form of an amendment to the existing SDI statute, however, which does not explicitly offer job protection to workers while they are on disability leaves, the PFL bill was silent on the question of job protection. Pragmatists in the coalition also feared that including a job protection provision in the bill would provoke insurmountable opposition from employers.

Kuehl formally introduced the PFL bill in February 2002 and publicly stated that it would be her top priority for that year's legislative session. She assigned a talented member of her staff, Jennifer Richard, to work intensively on the bill. By mid-June 2002 it had been passed in the state Senate without any significant changes, to the surprise and pleasure of the advocates, who had expected a more drawn-out effort before reaching this stage in the legislative process.

For the previous year and a half the Coalition had been steadily building support in the wider community, reaching out to a variety of constituencies. It also organized a media training session for Coalition members in March 2002, correctly anticipating that the media would play a critical role in determining the final outcome of the campaign. Once the bill had passed the Senate and was sent to the Assembly for consideration, the Coalition's grassroots and media mobilization escalated to a new level of intensity. At this point, when the bill seemed to have a real prospect of becoming law, the business lobby began gearing up to oppose it. The countercampaign was led by the California Chamber of Commerce, which sent legislators thousands of letters communicating their opposition, insisting that businesses—especially small businesses—would be driven out of the state if PFL became law. They objected especially strongly to the tax on employers, arguing that businesses could not afford to pay it. They also contended that companies would face great difficulties in covering the work of employees while they were on family leave, incurring extra costs for overtime and for hiring and training replacement workers. In addition, the business lobby expressed concern that workers would abuse the program if it became law, filing fraudulent claims for paid leave.

In response to the growing pressure from the Chamber, a group of moderate, business-oriented Democrats proposed several key modifications to the PFL bill, most importantly eliminating the employer tax, a compromise to which Kuehl's office and the coalition soon agreed. The Labor Federation then took the position that if workers were going to shoulder the full cost of the program, the benefit should be cut back from twelve to six weeks; so that amendment was also made in the Assembly version of the bill. Another new provision that the business-oriented Democrats requested specified that employers could require workers to use up to two weeks of paid vacation time (if available) before receiving PFL. Thus amended, the bill was passed by the state Assembly on August 27, 2002, by a comfortable margin; three days later the Senate passed the amended version and the bill went to Governor Davis's desk. At the time he was up for reelection in what was expected to be a tight race, a factor that may well have worked in the advocates' favor, given the broad popular support for PFL.

During the month of September, with no clear signals of the governor's intentions, PFL advocates intensified their grassroots organizing and media outreach, generating a blitz of letters, faxes, and e-mails directed at the governor, urging him to sign PFL into law. The Coalition also persuaded high-profile political leaders and celebrities from all over the country to contact Davis, highlighting the historic significance of the bill, which would bring into existence the nation's first comprehensive paid family leave program. Once the tax on employers was eliminated, the business objections lost much of their previous credibility with the public, and the PFL bill won endorsements from some major newspapers.

The Coalition by this time had mushroomed to include over seven hundred organizations and individuals. In addition to organized labor, there were advocates for seniors such as the American Association of Retired Persons (now the AARP), the Gray Panthers, and the Older Women's League; women's organizations such as the state branch of the National Organization for Women, the California Women's Law Center, Planned Parenthood, and the American Association of University Women; advocates for children and childcare such as Children NOW, the Children's Advocacy Institute, and the Childcare Resource and Referral Network; organizations of medical practitioners such as the American Academy of Pediatrics, the American College of Obstetricians and Gynecologists, and the California Medical Association; and several faith-based groups as well as an assortment of other progressive organizations.[13]

The breadth of the Coalition, which included many powerful organizations with large constituencies backing them up, was a crucial element in the campaign's success in overcoming the business lobby's opposition to the PFL bill. Labor's support, while crucial, was not enough, in part because Governor Davis had previously signed several other bills that labor supported, which diminished the leverage of the state Labor Federation in relation to PFL at this final stage in the process. With this in mind, advocates now spotlighted women's strong interest in paid leave, signaling the issue's broad public appeal to Davis as he considered whether or not to sign the bill in the context of his upcoming reelection campaign. The Coalition's arguments also emphasized that PFL would help a wide range of Californians at all income levels, and would benefit newborns as well as the frail elderly. Another key selling point was that PFL was a revenue-neutral measure, the modest costs of which would be borne entirely by employees, building on an established program (SDI) that had a track record of success.

The Coalition was armed with strategic capacity, vital data in support of PFL, and a broad-ranging set of organizational and individual supporters that mobilized on behalf of the bill. All of this was critical to the campaign's success. But another essential element was the way in which the issue was framed in the public debate and especially in the media, as an in-depth study by Lori Dorfman and Elena O. Lingas (2003) of the print media coverage of the PFL campaign later documented in detail. It found that advocates avoided getting bogged down in technical details about the proposed program and instead concentrated their campaign rhetoric on the basic human needs that PFL would serve—an approach that proved highly effective. Indeed, the single most common framing of the issue by PFL advocates focused on the ways in which paid leave would provide workers with the opportunity to care for loved ones and allow parents to bond with newborn babies. This frame was present in over two-thirds (69%) of the print media pieces the study analyzed. The second most common framing (in 41% of the media pieces) similarly emphasized the human needs PFL would meet, emphasizing that in its absence workers were being forced to chose between their families and their jobs (Dorfman and Lingas 2003, 6–7, 21).

Significantly, Dorfman and Lingas found, the opposition never challenged these core arguments put forward by the advocates. Rather than suggesting that bonding with newborns or caring for sick family members was somehow problematic, opponents framed their arguments against PFL primarily around claims that it would impose an unfair burden on businesses, especially small businesses. A closely related framing was the assertion that PFL's passage would put the state at a competitive disadvantage. These were the two most common opposition frames, appearing in 59 percent and 30 percent of the print media stories the study analyzed, respectively. In both framings the "job killer" label appeared repeatedly (Dorfman and Lingas 2003, 9).

PFL advocates also put forward a "business case" for PFL. The Coalition was able to identify a few business owners who supported the bill, and persuaded them to speak out. For example, Paul Orfalea, the founder of Kinko's, wrote a letter to the editor of the *Santa Barbara News Press* entitled "Paid Leave: $2 a Month; Happy Workers: Priceless." Another supporter was Elliott Hoffman, cofounder of a small business in Oakland, Just Desserts, who declared that PFL was "a no-risk bill."[14] In September, just days before Davis signed the bill, the Coalition held a teleconference of pro-PFL business spokespeople, which attracted some media attention (Dorfman and Lingas 2003, 17). However, the vast majority of business lobbyists opposed the bill at every stage of the campaign, even after the advocates had agreed to eliminate the payroll tax on employers and make other amendments to address the stated concerns of the opposition. It became clear that the Chamber simply could not be appeased. Even in the Democratic-dominated political climate that existed in California in 2002, this was a formidable obstacle to overcome.

Blessed with an exceptionally favorable political climate, however, the advocates successfully outflanked the powerful business lobby. They built an extensive grassroots and interest-group rich coalition that was actively mobilized in support of the PFL bill, and they focused their rhetoric squarely on the key human needs the proposed program would address, without getting trapped in technicalities or expending a lot of effort debating the issue on the terms set by the business lobby's "job killer" frame. Thus the advocates carried the day, and Governor Davis signed the bill into law on September 23, 2002. In the election campaign that immediately followed, he often mentioned PFL in his speeches and campaign advertisements; he would later highlight it as one of his most important accomplishments as governor. Moreover, a year later when Arnold Schwarzenegger replaced Davis as governor in the dramatic October 2003 recall election, he made no effort to eliminate the PFL program (which had not yet begun operating), in implicit recognition of its widespread popular support.[15] The California business community, too, although expressing dismay at its defeat immediately after the bill was signed (Jones 2002), soon moved on, just as it had with FMLA. As we show in chapter 4, companies would find it very easy to adjust to the change, and many of them benefitted from the new PFL program once it went into effect. Before exploring the program's impact on business in further detail, however, we turn to briefly examine the way in which PFL has been implemented and administered, as well as the extent to which California employees have made use of it since July 1, 2004, when it first began operations.

3

CHALLENGES OF LEGISLATIVE
IMPLEMENTATION

Soon after the legislation creating California's paid family leave program was passed, the focus shifted from the political arena to the more mundane but equally critical challenges of implementation and administration. This involved a series of distinct and highly demanding tasks. Regulations had to be drafted and disseminated, specifying in detail how the program would function. Administrative mechanisms, including claims-processing procedures, had to be created and tested. That task was simplified because PFL was so similar in structure to the existing SDI program and administered by the same agency, yet it still presented challenges. In addition, staff had to be recruited and trained to handle the large number of claims that was anticipated. Enforcement, an ongoing issue with FMLA (Kelly 2010; Gerstel and Armenia 2009), was another concern, although a relatively minor one in the case of PFL, since workers would apply directly to the state for benefits; employers' main legal obligation was simply to inform their employees about the program's existence.[1] Finally, there was a need to make workers, employers, and the general public aware of PFL—a new social insurance benefit available to over twelve million California workers.

The PFL law was passed in the autumn of 2002, more than a year before payroll deductions were scheduled to begin, on January 1, 2004; benefit payments would start six months later, on July 1, 2004. Although that seemingly provided ample time to prepare for launching the program, a series of delays and other logistical problems arose. For example, the necessary regulations were not completed until June 2004, only a month before benefit payouts began. Moreover, by 2004 the state of California was mired in a budget crisis, which led to a freeze on new spending and hiring, presenting added challenges for the Employment Development Department administrators responsible for running the new PFL program. Some of them purchased staplers, pens, and other supplies with their own personal funds, and they hired staff from an EDD "surplus list" because of the freeze. Under these difficult conditions, a team of dedicated EDD managers worked exceptionally long hours in early 2004 to meet the various deadlines for the program's implementation. One of them later compared PFL's infancy to that of a newborn baby, recalling that she would awaken in the wee hours each night worrying about it, and that she and her colleagues even composed songs about the program during this period.

Another issue arose soon after the PFL legislation was passed, when the U.S. Internal Revenue Service determined that PFL benefits would be subject to income tax—a finding that EDD formally disputed, although the agency's effort to reverse the IRS decision ultimately proved unsuccessful. This was an unexpected development, as SDI benefits had never been deemed taxable; nor is PFL subject to state income tax.

Programming the computerized PFL claims-processing system was a complex task and became another source of significant delays. Training the claims-processing staff was already well under way before the automated system was ready, and when it finally did begin operating various technical problems surfaced. Soon after the system was launched, some ten thousand claims mysteriously disappeared, or as the staff said, were "dropped by the robot." At another point, an administrator recalled, eight thousand claims got stuck in an "exceptions queue," creating so much extra work that staff members had to put in overtime for twenty-one days in a row.[2] Some technology issues persisted long afterward, most importantly that until late 2012 claimants could not apply for PFL online (Firestein, O'Leary, and Savitsky 2011, 14).

Despite the budget crisis and the difficult conditions it created, EDD's management team successfully addressed all of these challenges, and most of them were resolved in a relatively short period of time. Indeed, by all accounts the PFL program is administered efficiently and effectively, with few complaints from claimants. The application process is simple and straightforward. It involves a two-page form, which must be submitted to EDD along with supporting documentation—a birth certificate or other evidence of the claimant's relationship to the child for bonding claims, or a physician's certification of the medical condition of the ill family member for caregiving claims.

In our 2009–10 survey of five hundred Californians who had experienced events that made them eligible for PFL (see appendix for details), the vast majority of respondents who had used the program reported that they found it easy to access and that their claims were processed in a timely manner. Asked to rate the difficulty of filling out the claim form on a scale of 0 to 10, with 0 being "extremely easy," nearly a third (31%) of the respondents who had applied for PFL rated it 0 while almost three-quarters (73%) rated it in the 0 to 3 range; only 16 percent rated it 6 or higher. Moreover, among the subset of respondents who were aware of PFL but chose not to apply for it when they needed a leave, only 18 percent cited the hassles of filling out the application as one of the reasons they did not apply. Two-thirds (67%) of the respondents who had used the program reported that their applications were approved within two weeks, with only 8 percent reporting a wait of more than a month. And most respondents received their first PFL check promptly as well, with 60 percent reporting that it arrived within two weeks after their application was approved; only 8 percent had to wait a month or more before the first check arrived.

Making the public aware of the program has been a more difficult challenge, however. EDD launched a yearlong outreach program shortly after the PFL legislation was passed, designed to inform eligible workers about the new benefit. Billboards promoting PFL were erected on major freeways and near hospitals across the state. Brochures and posters were distributed, in multiple languages, and the agency reached out directly to clinics and community centers statewide as well. However, only $1 million in funding was available for this initial public education effort, and thereafter funds for continuing outreach about the program were even more limited. Many of the work-family advocates who led the campaign to pass the PFL legislation have supplemented the state's effort with their own outreach and education programs, and some run hotlines and legal clinics as well, but these groups' resources are far too limited to close the gap.

EDD's managers have maintained a strong and cooperative relationship with stakeholders in the work-family advocacy community from the program's outset. Quarterly meetings about PFL are convened by EDD administrators and attended by representatives of women's organizations, legal advocates, unions, caregiver and senior organizations, childcare advocates, and a variety of other grassroots community groups, as well as legislative staffers. This partnership has helped the agency identify implementation problems on the ground, and has served as a source of innovative approaches to outreach as well. For example, when the advocates suggested that EDD routinely send information about PFL, along with a claim form, to all workers who receive SDI pregnancy benefits, the agency made that standard operating procedure (Firestein, O'Leary, and Savitsky 2011, 13).

Despite all these efforts, however, public awareness of PFL remains limited, especially among those who could potentially benefit the most from using it—young workers, immigrants, low-wage workers, and disadvantaged racial and ethnic minorities. In 2003, a year after the bill creating PFL became law, a survey that we conducted found that only 22 percent of adult Californians were aware of the new program. Our follow-up survey in the summer of 2005, one year after PFL benefits began to be paid, found that awareness had increased to just below 30 percent of adult Californians. A third survey that we conducted in 2007 found an awareness level of 28 percent, although the drop from 2005 is not statistically significant. Awareness of PFL among Californians was much lower than awareness of related federal and state programs: in our 2007 survey, 55 percent of respondents were aware of FMLA and 69 percent knew about California's longstanding SDI program—in both cases, roughly double the level of PFL awareness.[3] Another survey conducted in 2005–06 of employed parents of chronically ill children in California found even lower PFL awareness levels: only 18 percent of them knew about PFL (Shuster et al. 2008). As we show in chapter 5, there is evidence that awareness of PFL has increased more recently, but it remains unequally distributed across the state's population and still lags far behind awareness of FMLA and SDI.

PFL Features and Coordination with Other Family Leave Laws

Even those who are aware of PFL may not fully understand the details of the program and how it interacts with the complex set of preexisting federal and state laws addressing pregnancy disability and family and medical leave that we enumerated in chapter 2, or how PFL can be coordinated with employer-provided paid leave benefits. Extensive information about PFL is available on the EDD website, and the agency also maintains a toll-free hotline that helps to answer questions about the program. California law requires all state agencies to provide services in English and Spanish; in the case of the PFL hotline five other languages are also offered (Cantonese, Vietnamese, Armenian, Punjabi, and Tagalog). Work-family advocacy groups have helped educate potential PFL recipients about the details of the program as well. For employers, ironically, the single best source of information is the California Chamber of Commerce. Although the Chamber had strongly opposed the passage of the law creating PFL, immediately after losing that battle the organization began developing educational materials to help employers understand their obligations in relation to the program and to clarify for them the ways in which PFL dovetails with other state and federal laws.[4] Still, confusion persists among employers and workers alike about which types of leaves are job-protected, how to manage transitions from one type of leave to another, and the extent to which multiple benefits can be used simultaneously.

One early concern involved a change in the name of the benefit, from the original Family Temporary Disability Insurance to Paid Family

Leave. The latter term has the virtue of simplicity but may have inadvertently created the impression that the program offers job-protected leaves; in fact it offers only partial wage replacement during specific types of family leaves—either for bonding with a new child or for caring for a seriously ill child, parent, spouse, or domestic partner. The limited list of family members eligible for care under PFL leaves is another potential source of confusion. The program does not provide wage replacement for workers who are caring for seriously ill siblings, in-laws, grandparents, or grandchildren—a serious limitation in a historical era when family structure is undergoing rapid change. One researcher found that about 10 percent of rejected PFL claims had been filed for leaves to care for individuals who were not included in the statute's definition of a family member (Sherriff 2007, 6).

The basic rules governing use of PFL are straightforward, but claimants may or may not be aware of all of them. Employers are legally required to notify newly hired workers and those who are planning to go on leave that they may be eligible for PFL, and to display an EDD-provided poster in the worksite that includes information about PFL (along with information about unemployment insurance and SDI). But employers are neither required to inform their employees in detail about the program nor to assist them in applying for it. Workers may be unaware that PFL leave may be taken on an intermittent rather than continuous basis; the minimum leave unit is one day, but workers may spread their PFL benefits over a twelve-month period if they so choose. They may or may not be aware that there is a waiting period of seven calendar days, during which the claimant does not receive PFL benefits. The one exception is for birth mothers who have also used SDI's pregnancy disability benefits, for which they have already been subject to a similar waiting period; they can receive PFL immediately after the SDI benefit runs out. Most important, because the new program does not provide any job protection, employers have no obligation to notify workers that taking a leave may lead to their termination.

Workers may not receive SDI and PFL benefits simultaneously, nor can they draw on PFL simultaneously with unemployment insurance or workers' compensation benefits. Finally, for any period of leave during which workers continue to receive their normal wages or salary, they may not draw on PFL, the purpose of which is to replace lost wages. Employers also may require their employees to use up to two weeks of accrued paid vacation time before taking up PFL. On the other hand, employers can choose to "top off" the state-provided PFL benefits, so long as the sum total of PFL and other payments from the employer does not exceed workers' normal pay. For example, an employer may permit the use of paid sick leave or paid vacation (or both), or some other type of family leave benefit to supplement PFL during an eligible leave.

Another complex issue involves job protection or the lack thereof. Neither PFL nor SDI provides any rights to continued employment or benefits, or to reinstatement at the end of a covered leave. But many workers do have such rights under Pregnancy Disability Leave (PDL) or FMLA/CFRA. As we saw in chapter 2, only about half the workforce meets the eligibility requirements for FMLA/CFRA, but those who do are entitled to up to twelve weeks of unpaid family leave in a twelve-month period, which may be taken on a continuous or intermittent basis. During a FMLA/CFRA covered leave taken for purposes of bonding with a new child or caring for a qualifying family member who is seriously ill, workers may receive PFL benefits. FMLA/CFRA covered workers also have rights to continuing health benefits while on leave for up to twelve weeks (although they may be required to pay their share of the premiums), as well as continuing seniority and pension accrual rights, if these existed prior to the leave. FMLA/CFRA covered workers also have the right to reinstatement in the same or a comparable position at the end of a leave of twelve weeks or less, except for a rarely invoked exemption involving "key employees" (salaried employees in the highest-paid 10 percent of the workforce whose reinstatement would cause "substantial and grievous economic injury" to the employer's operations).

California's PDL law covers a much larger population of workers than FMLA/CFRA. Any employer with five or more workers is covered by PDL, and workers are eligible from the date they are hired. PDL provides up to four months of job-protected unpaid leave—continuous or intermittent—for workers disabled by pregnancy, childbirth, or a related condition. PDL leaves require medical certification of disability, which for normal pregnancies is typically provided for a period of six to eight weeks; in complicated pregnancies a longer period (up to four months) of PDL leave may be certified. PDL leaves are unpaid, except in cases where employers' policy or practice is to pay workers during other types of disability leave.[5] After a PDL leave, with rare exceptions, workers are entitled to reinstatement to the same or a comparable position, with the same pay, benefits, and seniority rights and benefits they had before the leave began.[6]

The ways in which PFL, FMLA/CFRA, SDI, and PDL leaves are scheduled, and the extent to which they do or do not overlap, is a complicated issue that has been challenging for employers and workers alike to understand. Figure 3.1 depicts two common timelines for FMLA/CFRA covered workers (all of whom are also covered by PDL) who use PFL for (a) a birth mother's pregnancy disability and baby bonding leave or (b) a bonding leave for a parent other than a birth mother (this could be a father, a domestic partner of the birth mother, or an adoptive or foster parent), or any PFL-eligible leave to care for a seriously ill family member.

In the first example (figure 3.1a), the pregnant employee is eligible for PDL for ten weeks, which runs concurrently with FMLA. For nine of those weeks she is also entitled to receive SDI pregnancy disability benefits (except during the first week in the timeline, which is the SDI waiting period). She can activate CFRA's baby bonding leave provision starting in the eleventh week of her leave; at that point she can also start to collect PFL benefits. Here PDL and CFRA do not run concurrently but consecutively (but FMLA runs concurrently with them both, as depicted in the diagram). In this case the birth mother has a total of twenty-two weeks of job-protected leave, for fifteen of which she can receive partial wage replacement (nine weeks from SDI and six from PFL).

In the second, much simpler example, FMLA/CFRA runs concurrently with PFL, which provides 6 weeks of partial wage replacement. The employee may also be required to use up two weeks of accrued paid vacation (which runs concurrently with the one-week waiting period required under the PFL program) before receiving PFL benefits. In this case the worker has a total of twelve weeks of job-protected leave, up to eight of which are partially paid (up to two weeks from accrued vacation pay and six from PFL). There are many other possible scenarios depending on

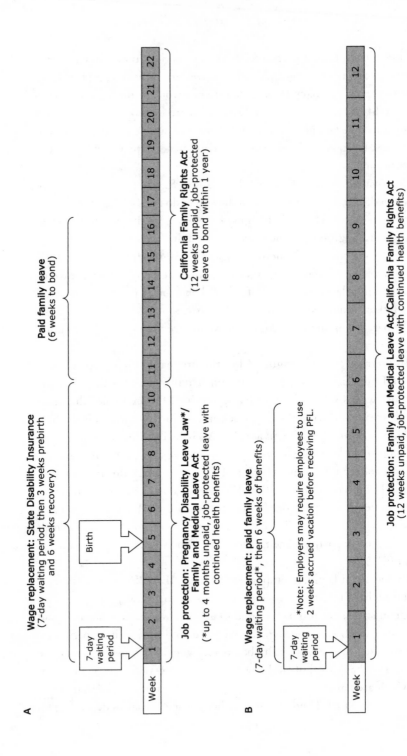

Figure 3.1. Possible timelines combining PFL with PDL, FMLA/CFRA, and/or SDI leaves: (A) Pregnancy disability and bonding leave for FMLA/CFRA eligible birth mother. (B) Caregiving and non-birth-parent bonding leave for FMLA/CFRA eligible worker. Courtesy of the Legal Aid Society–Employment Law Center.

A

Wage replacement: State Disability Insurance
(7-day waiting period, then 3 weeks prebirth
and 6 weeks recovery)

Paid family leave
(6 weeks to bond)

Week | 1 | 2 | 3 | 4 | 5 | 6 | 7 | 8 | 9 | 10 | 11 | 12 | 13 | 14 | 15 | 16 | 17 | 18 | 19 | 20 | 21 | 22

7-day waiting period

Birth

California Family Rights Act
(12 weeks unpaid, job-protected
leave to bond within 1 year)

**Job protection: Pregnancy Disability Leave Law* /
Family and Medical Leave Act**
(*up to 4 months unpaid, job-protected leave with
continued health benefits)

B

Wage replacement: paid family leave
(7-day waiting period*, then 6 weeks of benefits)

Week | 1 | 2 | 3 | 4 | 5 | 6 | 7 | 8 | 9 | 10 | 11 | 12

7-day waiting period

*Note: Employers may require employees to use
2 weeks accrued vacation before receiving PFL.

Job protection: Family and Medical Leave Act/California Family Rights Act
(12 weeks unpaid, job-protected leave with continued health benefits)

individual situations, but these examples illustrate two of the most common scenarios and expose the complexity of the overlap among the various laws involved. For those workers who lack coverage under FMLA/CFRA, the situation is far simpler: birth mothers do have job protection for the period in which they are collecting SDI pregnancy disability benefits, but not during any subsequent bonding leave for which they may draw on PFL. But workers who are not birth mothers and who lack FMLA/CFRA coverage have no job protection at all when they use PFL for either bonding or care leaves.

PFL Take-up Rates and Their Demographic Characteristics

Since the program began operating in 2004, PFL take-up rates have been substantially lower than early projections suggested. We have already touched on two of the reasons for this: the limited awareness of PFL among those eligible and the lack of job protection under the statute. Another likely contributing factor is the fact that wage replacement under PFL is partial—55 percent up to a cap of $1,011 per week in 2012, and subject to federal income tax. However, as table 3.1 shows, PFL take-up has increased over time. In the fiscal year ending in mid-2012, over 210,000 claims were filed (95% of which were paid), up from 150,000 in the program's first year of operations. A total of

TABLE 3.1.   Paid family leave claims, by type and length, 2004–11

Fiscal Year	2004–05	2005–06	2006–07	2007–08	2008–09	2009–10	2010–11	2011–12
Total claims	150,514	160,988	174,838	192,494	197,638	190,743	204,893	210,167
Bonding claims	132,007	141,319	153,120	168,594	175,406	167,523	178,853	183,421
Care claims	18,507	19,669	21,718	23,900	22,232	23,220	26,040	26,746
Weeks/ claim	4.84	5.35	5.37	5.35	5.39	5.37	5.30	5.35

Source: State of California, Employment Development Department.

nearly 1.5 million PFL claims were filed in the eight years shown in the table.

The vast majority (87%–89%) of each year's claims were for bonding with a new child, as table 3.1 shows; this reflects the fact that awareness that the program can be used for family caregiving is even more limited than awareness of the program generally (as we document in chapter 5). The percentage of employees covered by PFL who filed claims has increased slightly over the life of the program, but remains below 2 percent of the total number of eligible employees. This is not only due to limited awareness of the program but also reflects the fact that the life events that make workers eligible for the program (a new child or a seriously ill family member) are infrequent occurrences. Most workers will experience such an event at some point in the course of their working lives, but at any given point in time only a small proportion of the workforce will do so. Table 3.1 also shows that PFL claims average just over five weeks, slightly less than the maximum of six weeks available under the program. (This reflects the fact that the vast majority of claims are for baby bonding; care leaves tend to be shorter.)

TABLE 3.2. Percentage distribution of PFL claimants and PFL-eligible workers, by individual earnings bracket, California, 2010

Annual earnings ($)	Total PFL claims (%)	PFL-eligible workers (%)
0–12,000	5.9	16.5
12,001–24,000	18.2	21.6
24,001–36,000	18.8	18.9
36,001–48,000	14.7	12.0
48,001–60,000	10.9	9.7
60,001–72,000	7.5	4.9
72,001 or more	24.1	16.4
Total	100.0	100.0

Sources: State of California, Employment Development Department; U.S. Current Population Survey, 2011 March Supplement.
Notes: PFL claims include both bonding and care claims for the fiscal year July 1, 2010 to June 30, 2011, distributed by earnings in the base period of the previous year. The PFL-eligible workers data shown in the rightmost column is for calendar year 2010 and include all California private-sector workers, excluding the self-employed, who worked at least fourteen weeks and ten hours in that year. Totals may not add to 100% due to rounding.

Table 3.2 compares the distribution of PFL claimants and PFL-eligible workers by earnings level in 2010. It shows that low-wage workers (those with annual earnings of $12,000 or less) were underrepresented among those taking up PFL, relative to the eligible workforce, while high earners (those with annual earnings over $72,000) were overrepresented. Workers at other earnings levels took advantage of the PFL program in similar proportions to their share of the eligible workforce. This confirms the results of an earlier analysis by the California Senate Office of Research, based on data from the first two years of PFL's operation.[7] That study also found that individuals who worked for large employers (those with one thousand or more employees) were overrepresented among PFL claimants. Such workers accounted for nearly half the claims in the program's first two years of operation, even though only about 14 percent of the workforce is employed in these large organizations (Sherriff 2007, 7, 9).[8] As we discuss in more detail in chapter 5, this suggests that the PFL program has not yet done much to alter the regressivity of access to paid leave that existed previously.

Another striking trend in the PFL take-up data is that the percentage of males filing bonding claims has grown steadily and substantially since PFL benefits became available. As figure 3.2 shows, the male percentage of care claims has been consistently higher than the male percentage of bonding claims from the outset, and male PFL take-up rates for purposes of caring for a seriously ill family member have changed little over the life of the program. In contrast, however, male take-up of PFL for bonding purposes has grown dramatically. As a result, the gap in the male percentage of claimants between the two types of leave has narrowed greatly.

PFL benefits are available equally to both men and women who become new parents or who have an eligible family member with a serious medical condition. And since eligibility for PFL is based on past employment, regardless of gender, both men and women who actively participate in parenting a new child can take advantage of the program, either sequentially or at the same time. Similarly, both males and females may act as caregivers for an ill spouse, parent, child, or domestic partner, so long as no more than three eligible family members are receiving PFL for providing care for a given individual in any twenty-four-hour period. The

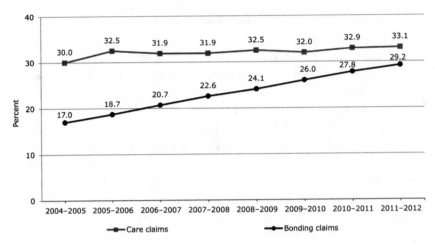

Figure 3.2. Percentage of PFL claims filed by men, by type of claim, California, 2004–12. Data from State of California, Employment Development Department.

fact that PFL offers wage replacement during family leaves (in contrast to FMLA/CFRA's unpaid leaves) seems to have provided an effective incentive for men's increased participation in caregiving, both for fathers who are bonding with their children and for those caring for seriously ill family members. Women still use the PFL program for bonding to a much greater extent than men do, but as figure 3.2 shows, men's PFL bonding claims have grown by over 12 percentage points over the brief life of the program.[9] By 2011–12, men comprised nearly a third of all claimants for both care and bonding leaves.

Our 2009–10 survey of California workers who had experienced events eligible for PFL (either becoming parents or having a seriously ill family member) found a male take-up rate similar to that shown in figure 3.2, although the survey only captured one point in time. Among respondents who were aware of PFL and employed in the private or nonprofit sector, 25 percent of males and 49 percent of females had made use of the PFL program. Although among these respondents women took longer leaves than men did, the men who did go on leave took substantial time off (whether they used PFL or not): their median leave length was three weeks for both bonding and caregiving leaves, compared to a median of twelve weeks for women's bonding leaves and five weeks for women's caregiving leaves.

The employers we surveyed in early 2010 (see chapter 4 and appendix for details) also reported an increase in male workers taking parental leaves following PFL's implementation. Asked if "the number of men who took paid parental leave this year to care for a new child is more, less, or about the same as it was five years ago," 31 percent of our employer respondents said "more," while only 5 percent said less (the remainder reported no change). Many of these employers also reported that men, like women, were taking longer leaves than before PFL was available: 32 percent of employer respondents indicated that men were taking longer parental leaves than before, compared to 4 percent who indicated that men were taking shorter leaves (the others reported no change). Employer respondents reported an average parental leave for men of four weeks, compared to ten weeks for women.

We heard many comments from managers about fathers taking longer parental leaves in our fieldwork as well. "Women's and men's parental leaves have both become longer since the state PFL program began," a human resources manager at a large manufacturing firm told us. "Men used to take only two weeks off when they had a new child, using sick leave and/or vacation. Today new fathers typically take around five to six weeks of bonding leave." A human resources manager at a law firm, similarly, observed that in recent years fathers had begun taking longer parental leaves. "The word is out," she told us. At this company, which supplemented PFL with its own parental leave benefits, new fathers typically took leaves ranging from two weeks to three months. The manager commented, "I think it's a generation X, generation Y phenomenon."

As the data in this chapter show, the PFL program is now firmly in place and on the whole has been implemented successfully, overcoming numerous unexpected challenges that presented themselves at the outset. Two continuing concerns stand out, however: the limited awareness among Californians of PFL's availability, on the one hand, and the complexity of coordinating PFL with other state and federal laws providing rights to family leaves, on the other. As we will see in chapter 5, there are additional concerns as well, most important the fact that—in contrast to PFL's strikingly positive impact on *gender* inequality demonstrated by the increased male participation in caregiving discussed above, the program has thus far left the *class* gap in access to paid family leave almost untouched. Nevertheless, PFL already has benefited nearly 1.5 million California workers, providing them with greater economic security than most would otherwise have had access to when they needed to go on leave from their jobs to welcome a new child into their families or to care for a seriously ill relative. This in itself is a considerable achievement.

Paid Family Leave and California Business

Business opposition to the legislation that established California's paid family leave (PFL) program was ubiquitous in the months prior to its passage in the fall of 2002. Despite the fact that, in the final version of the law, workers' payroll tax contributions fully funded the program, with no direct costs to employers, business groups were unrelenting in their vehement opposition. The president of the California Chamber of Commerce singled the PFL bill out for special censure in the immediate aftermath of its passage, saying, "We've opposed a lot of bills, but this is one of the worst" (Broder 2002).

The business lobby repeatedly asserted that the new program was a "job killer" with the potential to wreak havoc on businesses in the state (Anderson 2002; Payne 2002). In a jointly written op-ed published in the *San Diego Union-Tribune* a year before PFL was scheduled to be fully implemented (but ten months after the law creating it had been passed), the presidents of the California Manufacturers and Technology Association, the California Chamber of Commerce, and the California

Business Roundtable denounced PFL as a "mega job-killing bill" (Stewart, Zaremberg, and Hauck 2003). The Chamber's president predicted that if PFL was implemented, businesses would lose control over their employees and that the costs associated with replacing absent workers would be prohibitive (Edds 2002). And a spokesperson for the National Federation of Independent Business declared that PFL would be the biggest financial burden imposed on the state's small businesses in decades (Geissinger 2002).

Among the criticisms of the program that business groups articulated was the fact that it did not require that employees have any minimum tenure in their jobs before becoming eligible to apply for leave, the lack of a "carve out" for small employers, and the notion that the program would transfer control over leave policies from employers to the state (Taylor 2002; Koss 2003). Another objection was that decisions about eligibility would be made by the Employment Development Department, the state agency that administers the PFL program, and not by employers (Girion and Garvey 2002).

Business also expressed alarm about the potential for fraud and abuse, noting that the law requires workers to certify that they have primary responsibility for caring for an ill family member, but provides no mechanism for either EDD or the employer to verify that this is true (Taylor 2002). "It's so easy for someone to say, 'Aunt Mary needs me to go take care of her,' and the decision whether that person is eligible for paid leave or not is going to be made by the Employment Development Department," one employer complained (Girion and Garvey 2002).[1] The business lobby also suggested that workers would try to take advantage of the PFL program to extend their vacations or to take additional time off whenever they could, and that the program would be abused in a variety of other ways by workers who lacked a legitimate need for family leave (Girion and Garvey 2002).

Moreover, a spokesperson for the state Chamber of Commerce argued that the indirect costs of PFL—such as overtime pay and training for coworkers who would need to cover the duties of those on leave, and hiring temporary replacements for absent workers—would be a crippling burden on California employers and workers (Geissinger 2002). Some business groups also professed concern about the tax burden the new program would impose on workers who, in the final version of the law, were fully responsible for financing PFL through payroll deductions. Prior to its passage, the California Chamber of Commerce estimated that PFL would cost $2.5 million a year, nearly four times the estimate advocates had put forward (Geissinger 2002). The president of the Ventura Chamber of Commerce predicted that adding PFL to the existing State Disability Insurance program would triple the payroll tax on employees (Taylor 2002).

These widely expressed fears regarding PFL's potentially negative effects on business have not materialized, however, as we document in the rest of this chapter. According to employers themselves, in the vast majority of cases PFL has had minimal impact on business operations. Although some organizations do incur additional expenses when covering the work of leave-takers, many more enjoy cost savings thanks to PFL. For the latter, the state benefit has replaced paid leave benefits employers had previously provided, thus generating savings. Moreover, insofar as PFL reduces turnover, it also generates savings for employers by reducing the considerable expenses of recruiting and training new workers. Fears of widespread abuse of the program have also proved unwarranted. And the cost of the program—which in any case is borne entirely by workers—turned out to be well below even the advocates' initial projections: the payroll tax in 2012 for the SDI and PFL programs combined—fully paid by employees—is only 1 percent of the first $95,585 of earnings.

In documenting the ways in which PFL has impacted California businesses, we draw on two types of original data, one quantitative and one qualitative. The quantitative data come from two telephone surveys we conducted with California employers, first in early 2004, after the PFL law had been passed but before the program was fully operational, and again in early 2010, more than five years after PFL was implemented. Each survey sample included over 250 establishments, and each was stratified by establishment size, so that we could test the prediction that the burden of PFL on small businesses would be particularly onerous.[2] This chapter also draws on data from our surveys of California employees before and after PFL was implemented (described in chapter 5 and in the appendix). In addition to the employer and employee surveys, we conducted interviews during site visits to a convenience sample of about twenty workplaces around the state, in a variety of industries and sectors. At each site we interviewed human resource managers or operations managers to learn about how they managed leaves on a day-to-day basis. This fieldwork provided a rich body of qualitative data complementing the quantitative data from the employer surveys. The timing was similar to that of the surveys: we did the first round of site visits in early 2004, after the PFL legislation had been passed but before the program was fully implemented; our follow-up visits took place in late 2009 and early 2010. Unlike the surveys, however, the fieldwork was longitudinal: whenever possible we did follow-up visits to the same workplaces, five and a half years after PFL was operational. This enabled us to examine the program's impact on a select group of employers in considerable detail.[3]

California Employers' Family Leave Policies before PFL

In the 2004 employer survey, we asked respondents about the extent to which they provided wage replacement in any form (paid sick leave, paid vacation, and paid parental leave, for example) for the types of family leaves—bonding or caring for a seriously ill family member—that the PFL program was about to make available. We were especially interested in comparing the benefits employers offered to "exempt" managers and professionals—those who are not covered by laws requiring overtime pay—with the benefits employers offered to other, "nonexempt" employees.[4] On average, respondents to the 2004 employer survey reported that 60 percent of their nonexempt employees and 72 percent of their exempt employees had received partial or full pay while on leaves of more than one week to care for a new child or a seriously ill family member during the year preceding the survey. In nearly all cases (for 93% of nonexempts and 92% of exempts) this took the form of paid sick leave, paid vacation, or "paid time off" (a benefit combining paid sick leave and paid vacation); very few of these employers had formal paid family leave programs. As figure 4.1 shows, workers in larger establishments (fifty or more workers) were more likely to have such benefits than those employed by smaller ones, although, regardless of establishment size, benefit provision tended to be more generous for exempt than nonexempt employees. Not surprisingly, establishments with unionized workers were more likely to offer such benefits than those with no union presence.

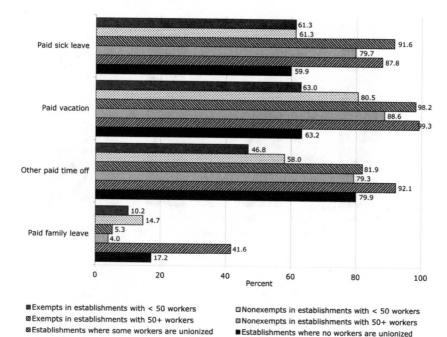

Figure 4.1. Employer-provided benefits, by selected characteristics of workers and establishments, California, 2004. N = 263. Authors' 2004 Employer Survey.

We also asked these employers about their experience with the 1993 Family and Medical Leave Act. Not all of them were fully aware of its provisions: among those with fifty or more employees, only 80 percent indicated that their employees were covered by FMLA, while another 14 percent were "not sure." (In fact under the law all establishments of that size are covered.) Among smaller establishments—many of which, though it is impossible to determine how many, were part of larger, covered firms—29 percent reported that they were covered by FMLA, while 39 percent of this group were "not sure." Those who indicated that FMLA did apply to their worksites were then asked to evaluate the effect of complying with it on productivity, profitability, turnover, and morale. The vast majority of them, as figure 4.2 shows, reported that FMLA had "no noticeable effect" on their organization. In regard to employee morale, moreover, most respondents who indicated that FMLA did have an effect evaluated it as

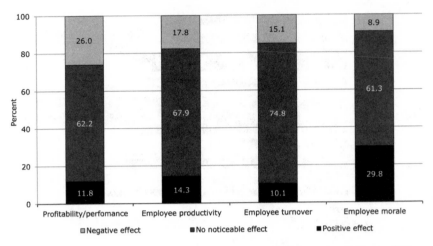

Figure 4.2. Effects of FMLA compliance on establishment performance, California, 2004. N = 163. Authors' 2004 Employer Survey.

positive, although in the other three areas those who perceived a negative effect slightly outnumbered those who perceived a positive one.[5]

These results echo those of a national U.S. Department of Labor employer survey conducted in 2000, seven years after FMLA became law, in which large majorities of employers reported that the 1993 law had "no noticeable effect" or a "positive effect" on productivity (84%), profitability (90%) or business growth (90%). In that 2000 survey, similar percentages of employers reported that intermittent FMLA leaves had "no noticeable effect" or a "positive effect" on productivity and profitability (U.S. Department of Labor 2001, tables 6.4, 6.5 and A2–6.13; Waldfogel 2001), although such intermittent leaves remain controversial. In our 2004 employer survey, very few respondents reported any experience of employee abuse of FMLA. When asked, "Have you ever had an employee take a leave under FMLA on a fraudulent basis?" less than 1 percent of the FMLA-covered respondents answered "yes," and more than half of that small group indicated that they had seen only one or two instances of such abuse in the previous year.[6]

We also asked managers about their experiences with FMLA in the first wave of site visits that we conducted in early 2004, prior to PFL's implementation. Table 4.1 summarizes their responses. Confirming the survey results, most interviewees reported that the effects of the federal law on their operations were positive or neutral. Several of them told us that FMLA pregnancy and bonding leaves, as well as medical leaves (as for nonemergency surgery) that could be scheduled in advance, were the easiest to manage, since advance planning was feasible—unlike leaves involving unanticipated medical crises, which took all concerned by surprise. But even in the latter cases, as a manager (case D) noted, "The problems are at the beginning; you have to scramble to figure out how to get the work done when someone first goes. After that, though, it's not a problem."

Several managers suggested that FMLA had not only helped them to retain valued employees but also had a positive impact on organizational morale in their workplaces. "The people who get the leaves appreciate it," one commented (case G, the corporate headquarters of a food company). "In the long term, we get better productivity, because employees feel they are supported by the company," another declared (case D, a computer engineering firm). "Overall, it helps with morale." Similarly, the human resource manager of an apparel retail chain (case K) noted, "Yes, people have the burden of picking up the slack for someone else on leave, but they also know that someone will do this for them if they need it." Another human resource manager told us, "It gives employees peace of mind, and plays into our [firm's] culture of work-life balance" (case O, a law firm). "Turnover would be much higher in the absence of FMLA leaves," an entertainment company human resource manager suggested (case F). "And other employees, coworkers, are sympathetic."

The one issue that several managers did complain about involved the intermittent leaves available under FMLA, which in some cases created time-consuming and annoying problems for managers. Especially difficult were situations where an employee could obtain blanket medical documentation of a chronic health condition, such as migraine headaches or asthma. This led to chronic and unpredictable absenteeism. "The migraines occur regularly on Monday or Friday or when it will be particularly busy," one frustrated manager explained (case S, a public utility). Another informant (a hospital manager at case C) told us, "The employee can just call up in the morning and not come in. It's unchecked, uncontrollable absenteeism. It's like they have a 'Get Out of Jail Free' card!" Such problems, although by all accounts limited to a handful of employees, not only were a nuisance

TABLE 4.1. Case studies, employer experience with FMLA leaves, California, 2004

Case code	Type of business	Total employees	Covered by FMLA?	Employees aware of FMLA	Employees return after FMLA leaves?	Effect of FMLA on organization
A	Manufacturing	1,500	Yes	Most are	Nearly all return	"No effect at all"
B	Software design	850	Yes	Yes	Most return	Positive effect on morale
C	Hospital	8,500	Yes	Yes	Nearly all return	Some abuse, especially with intermittent leaves; this reduces morale
D	Computer engineering	16,000	Yes	Yes	About 75% return	Improves productivity and morale
E	Optometrist	3	No	N/A	N/A	N/A
F	Entertainment	2,000	Yes	Yes	"Most people do"	Has reduced turnover
G	Food–headquarters	250	Yes	Yes	7 of 8 did last year	Mostly good for morale, but some abuse by a handful of employees
H	Food–agricultural work	1,400	Yes	Yes	Most return	No effect on morale, profitability, productivity
I	Food processing plant	120	Yes	Yes	Most return	Reduces turnover, no effect on morale, profitability or productivity
J	Insurance	2,652	Yes	Yes	85% return	No effect on turnover, profitability, or productivity

Case code	Type of business	Total employees	Covered by FMLA?	Employees aware of FMLA	Employees return after FMLA leaves?	Effect of FMLA on organization
K	Apparel retail chain	19,700	Yes	Yes	Most return	Positive impact on retention, negative for productivity and profitability
L	Computer chip design	12,500	Yes	Yes	Most return	No effect–a "nonevent"
M	Restaurant chain	550	Yes	Yes	90% or more return	"No big deal"
N	Biotechnology	97	Yes	Yes	Nearly all return	Positive effect on morale
O	Law firm	1,425	Yes	Yes	Over 90% return	Good for morale and recruitment
P	Construction/ engineering	850	Yes	Yes	Nearly all return	"We have it down pat." No effects
Q	Payroll processing	629	Yes	Yes	90% return	Overall, no effect
R	Nonprofit Research Firm	943	Yes	Yes	Everyone has returned	Positive for organization
S	Public utility	14,000	Yes	Yes	Nearly all return	Intermittent leaves that abuse law are bad for morale and productivity

for managers but could also spark resentment and thus morale problems among the coworkers of the employees involved.

Although intermittent leave issues were a serious concern for some employers, the problem was not widespread among the establishments we visited, and in some cases it was associated with broader problems of dissatisfaction and morale. At the public utility (case S), for example, one manager noted that intermittent leaves had become common in a department that also suffered from poor work organization and a work scheduling system that was the object of frequent employee complaints. After a new department supervisor was hired who put scheduling on a more rational and predictable basis, and who applied company rules in a fair and consistent manner, morale improved and absenteeism fell—as did the use of intermittent leave.

Most of the managers we interviewed felt that the positive benefits of FMLA outweighed its negative features, and some were positively enthusiastic. "You always have perfunctory whining from managers," one human resource manager told us (case R, a nonprofit research firm). "But everyone has problems from time to time and we understand that employees need time off occasionally." Another manager, who described himself as an advocate of work-life balance, defended the decade-old FMLA law against what he saw as ideological criticism from others in the business community. In his view, FMLA was a "nonevent" as far as productivity and profitability were concerned. "When we're talking about bottom-line issues, I've never heard anyone say, 'The real problem is FMLA.' No one has ever said, 'The share price of our stock stinks, and if we could only repeal this leave law we'd be doing better'" (case L).

PFL's Impact on Leave-taking Rates

One might expect that once PFL became available, California workers would take family leaves more often, and for longer periods of time, than before this form of wage replacement benefit was available. Indeed, we saw some evidence of this in chapter 3, which documented the increasing take-up of PFL among men for bonding leaves. On the other hand, the deep recession that began in 2007 has sharply increased employment insecurity, and may have made workers more hesitant than before to go on any type of extended leave, particularly among those whose right to return to the same or a comparable job is not legally protected. The data on rates of leave-taking and leave lengths (in tables 4.2 and 4.3, respectively) should be interpreted with these factors in mind.

Table 4.2 shows the rates of leave-taking that employers reported in our 2004 and 2010 surveys, and the variation in those rates by establishment size. In both years, more than half of the employers reported that *no* employees had taken parental leave in the previous year. In both the 2004 and 2010 surveys, more than 85 percent of small establishments (less than fifty employees) reported no cases of parental leave in the previous year; among those small establishments that did report at least one case of parental leave, the median rate of parental leave-taking was about 7 percent in both survey years, which translates into one employee per year in a typical establishment with twenty employees and three employees per year for one with forty to fifty employees. Of course, as the number of employees per establishment increases, the likelihood that at least one will go on a parental leave rises. Indeed, as table 4.2 shows, among establishments with 50 to 499 employees, 36 percent in 2004 and 38 percent in 2010 had at least one employee who took parental leave. As a share of the workforce at these worksites, however, median rates of parental leave-taking were miniscule: 1.4 percent in 2004 and 2.1 percent in 2010, which translates into about one employee a year for establishments with fifty employees and about ten a year for those with 499 employees. Among the largest establishments (five hundred or more employees), the likelihood that at least one employee will need to take parental leave during the year was still higher: 38 percent in 2004 and 82 percent in 2010. Here too, median rates of parental leave taking were modest, about 2 percent in both 2004 and 2010. What appears to be a higher rate of leave-taking in small establishments is largely an artifact of arithmetic: a worksite with only ten employees in which one takes parental leave will have a leave-taking rate of 10 percent.

As table 4.2 shows, between 2004 and 2010 there was a statistically significant increase—by a factor of two—in the number of parental leaves in the largest establishment category (establishments with five hundred or more employees). However, in all the other establishment size categories the change over time was not statistically significant, despite the establishment of PFL in the interim. The limited extent of change over this period may reflect the fact that birth rates decline in periods of economic downturn, or it may be an indication of workers' greater reluctance to take leave during difficult economic times, or both. Even in normal economic

TABLE 4.2.   Parental and pregnancy leave-taking rates, by establishment size, California, 2004 and 2010

	All employer respondents		Less than 50 employees		50–499 employees		500+ employees	
	2004	**2010**	**2004**	**2010**	**2004**	**2010**	**2004**	**2010**
Total N of all establishments	263	253	134	102	65	84	64	67
Number of establishments with any parental leaves in past year	101	92	13	8	37	32	51	52
Percentage of establishments with any parental leaves in past year (weighted)	15.4	8.8	13.9	7.0	36.0	38.1	38.1	82.1*
Median parental leave-taking rate (percentage of workers in establishments with any parental leaves in past year)	1.8	2.5	6.7	7.4	1.4	2.1	1.7	2.4
Number of establishments with any pregnancy leaves in past ear		111		16		40		55
Percentage of establishments with any pregnancy leaves in past year (weighted)		13.4		11.3		47.6		86.6
Median pregnancy leave-taking rate (percentage of workers in establishments with any pregnancy leaves in past year)		2.5		6.5		2.5		2.0

Source: Authors' 2004 and 2010 Employer Surveys.
* $p < .001$.

times, however, only a small number of workers will become parents at any one point in time (although most will do so at some point in their working lives).

The 2004 survey did not include questions about pregnancy leaves (for which wage replacement was already available through SDI at that time). But since PFL cannot be used for wage replacement for pregnancy leaves, there is no reason to expect significant change in such leaves over time, except as a result of the economic downturn. In any case, the rates for pregnancy leaves in 2010 were generally similar to those for bonding leaves.

TABLE 4.3.   Median length of family leave (in weeks) by leave type, gender, and exempt/nonexempt status, California, 2004 and 2009–10

	Baby bonding		Ill family member	
	2004	2009–10	2004	2009–10
N (all leave takers)	65	98	33	53
Exempt				
Male	3	3	3	4
Female	11	12	4	4.5
Nonexempt				
Male	3	3	3	3
Female	12	12	3	5.5*

Source: Authors' 2004 and 2009–10 Employee Surveys.
* $p < .05$.

In addition to its effect on the frequency of leave-taking by employees, one might expect the availability of PFL to increase the length of leaves, since workers can afford to take more time off with partial wage replacement than in its absence. However, as table 4.3 shows, the length of baby bonding leaves that respondents to our employee surveys reported did not change significantly between 2004 and 2009–10. For men, the median leave length, whether they held exempt or nonexempt jobs, was three weeks in both periods. The median length of baby bonding leaves taken by new mothers in nonexempt jobs also was the same in both periods, at twelve weeks. Only mothers in exempt jobs reported taking longer leaves in the later year, and this change was small and statistically insignificant (the median was twelve weeks in 2009–10 and eleven weeks in 2004). The median length of leave to care for an ill family member did increase for women in both exempt and nonexempt jobs, and for men in exempt jobs, but these changes were not statistically significant. The only statistically significant increase occurred among nonexempt women taking leaves to care for a seriously ill family member.

PFL's Effects on Organizational Performance

The 2010 employer survey explored the impact of PFL on various aspects of organizational performance. To an even greater degree than the results reported for FMLA in the 2004 survey, the data show that PFL had a minimal impact on the operations of California businesses. As figure 4.3 shows, nine out of ten respondents reported either positive effects or no effect of PFL on their establishments. When asked, "What effect has it [PFL] had on this location's business productivity?" 89 percent of employer respondents reported either a "positive effect" or "no noticeable effect." Similarly, when asked, "What effect has it had on this location's business profitability/performance?" an even higher percentage of employer respondents, 91 percent, reported that PFL had either a "positive effect" or "no noticeable effect."[7] As for employee turnover, 93 percent of the employers surveyed in 2010 reported that it had a "positive effect" or "no noticeable effect." And nearly all respondents said that the effect on morale was either positive or not noticeable.

Contrary to the claims of business groups that the PFL program would place an especially severe burden on small businesses, as table 4.4 shows, among the small minority of employers that did report negative effects, the larger establishments—those with more than five hundred employees—were *overrepresented*. This may reflect the fact that in larger establishments the organizational representatives who responded to our telephone survey tended to be more removed from the day-to-day management of family

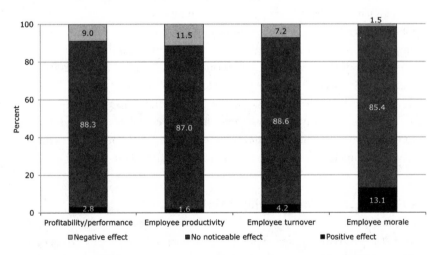

Figure 4.3. Effects of PFL compliance on establishment performance, California, 2010. N = 176. Totals may not add up to 100% due to rounding. Authors' 2010 Employer Survey.

leaves than those who responded on behalf of smaller establishments. It follows that some of the data shown in table 4.4 for the larger establishments may reflect ideologically rooted views of PFL rather than on-the-ground experience with leaves.

Our 2010 survey also explored another concern business groups had raised when the PFL legislation was being debated, namely that the program would be subject to abuse, with workers filing illegitimate claims. However, asked if they were "aware of any instances in which employees that you are responsible for abused the state Paid Family Leave program," 91 percent of all employer respondents surveyed replied "No." And among the other 9 percent who were aware of abuse, it was a relatively rare occurrence: 27 percent of them knew of only one instance of abuse, and 99 percent knew of no more than five such instances. Once again belying the concern that small businesses would be disproportionately affected by PFL, respondents from the largest establishments were more likely to report abuse than their smaller counterparts: 25 percent of establishments with five hundred or more workers reported abuse, compared to only 7 percent of establishments with fifty to 499 workers, and 9 percent in establishments with less than fifty workers (N = 177).

These survey findings about the impact of PFL on performance were confirmed in our fieldwork, when we returned in 2010 to the companies we had visited six years earlier to explore their experiences with the new state program.[8] Of the nineteen employers we visited in 2004, fifteen agreed to be reinterviewed in 2010. We replaced the other four (cases A, D, N, and Q in table 4.1) with similar companies in the same industry (these are denoted A', D', N', and Q' in tables 4.5, 4.8, and 4.9). As table 4.5 shows,

TABLE 4.4. PFL's effects on organizational performance, by establishment size, California, 2010 (%)

"Positive effect" or "no noticeable effect" on:	Less than 50 employees	50–499 employees	500+ employees	All employer respondents
Productivity	88.8	86.6	71.2	88.5
Profitability/performance	91.1	91.2	77.6	91.0
Turnover	92.2	98.6	96.6	92.8
Morale	98.9	95.6	91.5	98.6

Source: Authors' 2010 Employer Survey.
N = 175

TABLE 4.5. Case studies, employer experiences with PFL leaves, California, 2010

Case code	Type of business	Total employees	PFL's effects on organization
A'	Manufacturing	4,894	Small positive effect on profitability and morale. Employees really enjoy being able to spend more time with their new children. PFL has saved the company money since they now top off PFL.
B	Software design	2,781	N/A
C	Hospital	11,284	Minimal impact on productivity. Noticeable improvement in worker morale.
D'	Computer engineering	20,000	No effect on operations or productivity. Mothers love the program. Costs of PFL covered by payroll deductions, so there is no cost to the company.
E	Optometrist	4	No impact to date on the business, but concerned about potential future extended absences in this small business.
F	Entertainment	1,300	No negative impact. Boosts morale and company's "family oriented" image. Employees expressing gratitude for help with arranging leaves and "for caring."
G	Food– headquarters	1,334	No effect on productivity, profitability, turn-over, or absenteeism. "It's a blip on the radar screen."
H/I	Food–processing and agricultural work	1,000	No effect on operations. Workers less "stressed" over leave now that it is paid.
J	Insurance	2,000	No effect on the business.
K	Apparel retail chain	561	Not an issue for the company. PFL helps them retain employees.
L	Computer chip design	10,552	The cost of replicating PFL program as part of self-insurance SDI has been less than expected due to low take-up. Boosts morale.
M	Restaurant chain	630	No adverse impact. Coworkers like the opportunity to pick up extra shifts. Mothers like the additional income.
N'	Life sciences/ biotechnology	108	Long leaves can impact productivity– not PFL per se but long medical leaves. "It's a cost of doing business, but it's not a problem."

Case code	Type of business	Total employees	PFL's effects on organization
O	Law firm	270	"Stress" leaves incur resentment from coworkers. But for caregivers, it's better to take time off rather than working while distracted.
P	Construction/ engineering	810	No major impact on business or on turnover. Enables company to give new career hires rotational experience. "We use longer leaves to our advantage." Positively affects morale–coworkers help one another out, and PFL provides time to arrange childcare, reducing absenteeism.
Q'	Payroll processing	500	No effect, a "nonevent" for the company.
R	Nonprofit research firm	819	Overall it's positive, especially for retention. But parents more likely to take time off due to PFL income, and leaves are longer, especially for fathers. Gives employees a chance to rotate and get new skills and experience. Boosts morale.
S	Public utility	19,000	N/A
T'	Public-sector hospital	8,756	N/A

most of the managers we interviewed reported that PFL had had positive effects on their employees, especially in regard to morale (see cases C, F, P, and R). Several noted that employees themselves had very positive views of the program (cases A', D', M), and that employees' stress levels were reduced thanks to the availability of paid leave (cases H and M). Nearly all of these employers told us that the PFL program had had no negative effects on their business operations (cases D', E, F, G, H, J, K, M, P, Q') or a positive effect (cases A', P, and R). Only case C reported a minimal negative effect on productivity from family leaves. (At case N, managers also stated that long leaves impact productivity, but this involved medical leaves rather than family leaves.)

Covering the Work of Employees on Family Leave

The majority of employers we surveyed in 2010 reported that they typically covered the work of employees on leave by assigning the work temporarily to other employees. As table 4.6 shows, this was the primary method of covering the work of exempt workers on leave, cited by 77 percent of respondents. For an even larger proportion—90 percent—of these employers, this was the most common method of covering the work of nonexempt employees on leave. This practice was especially common in larger establishments, while in smaller ones the work of exempt employees was often put on hold, or employees were asked to do some work while they were out on leave. Many employers reported that they hired temporary replacements to cover the work of nonexempts during their leaves; this method was used a bit less frequently to cover the works of exempts.[9]

The widespread practice of assigning the work of an employee on leave to co-workers raises concerns that this might lead to resentment among

TABLE 4.6. Method of covering the work of family leave-takers, California, 2010 (%)

Method(s) used to cover the work of leave-takers	Exempt workers				Nonexempt workers			
	All establishments	Number of employees in establishment			All establishments	Number of employees in establishment		
		<50	50–499	500+		<50	50–499	500+
Assign work to others	76.9*	72.3	100.0	98.0	89.8	88.1	96.8	100.0
Hire temps	39.3	39.9	36.8	27.5	48.7	52.4	32.3	46.2
Hire replacements	0.4	0	0	3.9	2.4	0	12.9	1.9
Put work on hold	59.1**	67.5**	15.8	31.4	8.0	6.0	16.1	20.8
Workers do some work while on leave	45.5**	52**	13.2	5.9	6.6	6.0	9.7	1.9
Some other method	15.7	16.2	13.2	11.8	9.7	6.0	25.8	18.9

Source: Authors' 2010 Employer Survey.
Note: Totals may add up to more than 100% because employers could report more than one method.
N = 138
*p < .05; **p < .001, comparing exempt and nonexempt workers.

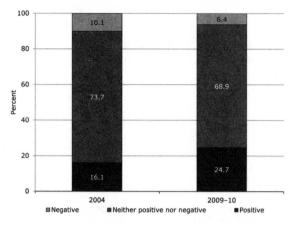

Figure 4.4. Impact of coworkers taking leave, California, 2004 and 2009–2010. N = 472 in 2004; N = 454 in 2009–10. Totals do not add up to 100% due to rounding. Authors' 2004 and 2009–10 Employee Surveys.

the latter group. We explored this question in the employee surveys in both 2004 and 2009–10; the results are summarized in figure 4.4 and table 4.7. In both years, about 60 percent of respondents had a coworker who went on leave. About a third of workers in each period reported working more hours as a result, and over half reported that they took on more duties. Although the great majority of workers reported that this had no impact or a positive impact in both years (90% in 2004 and 94% in 2009–10), the proportion reporting a positive impact increased from 16 percent in 2004 to 25 percent in 2009–10. Thus the concern that coworkers might resent having to fill in when a colleague goes on family leave turns out to be highly exaggerated. On the contrary, the view of employers that PFL improves worker morale is confirmed by these data on workers' views of leave-taking by coworkers.

Confirming the survey results, most of the employers we interviewed on our 2010 site visits told us that to cover the work of employees on leaves, they most often assigned the tasks involved to other employees, with the second most common method being hiring of temporary replacements to cover the work. These findings are summarized in table 4.8. In most of these companies, the work of employees on leave was covered by coworkers (cases A, B, D', F, H/I, M, N', O, P, and R). Some employers reported

TABLE 4.7. Rates and impacts of coworkers taking leave, California, 2004 and 2009–10

	2004	2009–10
Percentage of respondents with a coworker taking leave (%)	56.7	60.9
Effects of coworker leave on respondent's job (%)		
More hours	32.5	33.0
Extra shifts[a]	22.7	N/A
More duties	52.6	51.2
Overall impact of coworker taking leave on respondent (%)		
Positive	16.1	24.7*
Negative	10.1	6.4
Neither positive nor negative	73.7	68.9
N	264	278

Source: Authors' 2004 and 2009–10 Employee Surveys.
[a] 2009–10 survey did not include a question about extra shifts.
*p < .05, comparing 2004 to 2009–10.

the use of cross-training, opportunities for employees to learn new skills, and successful backup systems as among the key reasons they did not have to hire temps (cases B, H, K, and P). In a few cases, employers did regularly use temps (cases A, C, R); N' made occasional use of temps as well. And case H used overtime during peak demand periods to cover the work of those on leave. But assigning coworkers to cover the work was by far the most common approach.

At the same time, this apparent homogeneity of approaches obscures the rich variety of arrangements that were used for covering the work of employees during both brief and more extended absences. In our field-work, we found that every single employer we visited had developed systematic, and often ingenious, methods for covering the work of employees when they were absent for any extended period, whether it was for a family leave or for a vacation, or any other reason. As one might expect, there is considerable variation depending in part on the nature and urgency of the tasks that need to be covered.

In some settings, like a factory assembly line or a hospital, full coverage for all positions is needed 100 percent of the time. A hospital we visited

TABLE 4.8. Case studies, covering the work of employees on PFL leaves, California, 2010

Case code	Type of business	Total employees	Covering the work of employees on PFL leaves
A'	Manufacturing	4,894	Blue-collar work is covered by temps and white collar work by coworkers.
B	Software design	2,781	Coworkers cover the work. Many are cross-trained.
C	Hospital	11,284	Request a "traveler" for RNs, techs; for nurses, may also use trainees.
D'	Computer engineering	20,000	Coworkers cover; in the vast majority of cases, jobs are divided among work team.
E	Optometrist	4	Would be difficult to cover work in this small business.
F	Entertainment	1,300	Work is reassigned to other team members in a department.
G	Food–headquarters	1,334	N/A
H/I	Food–processing and agricultural work	1,000	In the fields, crews just run with fewer people. We use overtime in the peak season.
J	Insurance	2,000	Very few employees have taken leave.
K	Apparel retail chain	561	New hires cover sales work. High turnover means a job is available when employee returns from leave.
L	Computer chip design	10,552	Covered by coworkers.
M	Restaurant chain	630	They offer extra shifts to the rest of the workforce (but avoid paying overtime).
N'	Life sciences/ biotechnology	108	Mostly covered by coworkers, occasionally by temps.
O	Law firm	270	Developed a successful "back-up" system to avoid using temps.
P	Construction/ engineering	810	Work is reassigned to available coworkers.
Q'	Payroll processing	500	Many leave-takers are "virtual employees"–is good for moms.
R	Nonprofit research firm	819	Temps cover nonexempts' work; coworkers cover work of exempts.
S	Public utility	19,000	N/A
T'	Public-sector hospital	8,756	N/A (not covered by PFL)

(case T') provides one example of a situation where coverage is impera-
tive, and work is highly skilled. The hospital maintains a "voluntary extra
shift list" of nurses and nursing assistants, who indicate the days they are
available to work overtime. The hospital offers incentives for this by paying well above the legally mandated rate for overtime. Another approach
was used at the public utility (case S), where the work is also skilled and
often highly time sensitive. Here, managers rely on voluntary overtime
among coworkers to cover the work of employees who are absent. In one
manufacturing firm we visited, where one might expect hiring replacement workers or temps to be the main approach, the machine operators
worked in teams, enabling coworkers to be assigned to cover the work of
absent team members.

At the other end of the spectrum, as in office settings where deadlines
are typically more flexible, even absences of several months can be covered
by coworkers, with less urgent tasks put on hold and others taken over by
the staff that remain. In one worksite we visited, the corporate headquarters of a food manufacturing company, it is standard practice to put some
work on hold until the absent employee returns, while coworkers cover
the most urgent tasks. At a nonprofit research firm, similarly, coworkers
cover the duties of absent support staff; in some cases people are moved
from one office to another to balance workloads.

In retail chain stores and in agricultural work, where turnover is very
high and hiring is therefore virtually continuous, leaves can be handled
even more easily, since an employee's temporary absence can be covered by
one of the many new hires that are constantly arriving; and when a leave-
taker returns to work there is sure to be a position available. At the other
extreme, for jobs that require extensive training so that very few people
are able to take over for someone who is absent, managing leaves presents
a greater challenge and managers must be more inventive. At a law firm
we visited, where continual coverage of support staff positions is essential,
management keeps several floaters on the regular staff, drawing on temps
as a last resort. "Every day is a juggle," one manager said.

We also visited a small retail department within an entertainment company where merchandise is highly specialized. Here there were only four
full-time workers, but two other individuals with extensive training and
experience in this setting were available on an "on call" basis. These two
workers were not interested in working full time, but made themselves

available when the regular staff members were absent and occasionally have replaced a full-time worker on an extended leave. Similarly, a small branch of a restaurant chain that employs twenty-four nonexempt workers has four students on the payroll who work part-time and fill in when full-time staff members are unavailable.

At a biotechnology company we visited, extensive cross-training ensures that many professional and managerial employees can cover for one another during absences as needed. When this is not practical, the company employs contractors and consultants who periodically work for the firm and are generally familiar with its operations. A large engineering/ construction firm with a great deal of project-based work on tight deadlines adopted a different approach. Because professionals already routinely work very long hours, and because the price of engineering mistakes can be enormous, this firm does not ask coworkers to do additional work to cover for an absent engineer. Instead, management identifies another engineer within the firm who is working on a project that is winding down and assigns him or her to cover for the absentee. We observed a similar approach at a large high-tech firm that maintains a "redeployment" pool that includes both exempts (such as software engineers) and nonexempts (including factory workers as well as administrative support staff) whose positions had been eliminated. Managers regularly draw on this "redeployment" pool to find replacements for employees on leave.

The smallest business we visited, an optometrist's office, was the least well equipped to cover leaves. This business only has three employees (apart from the owner), one of whom is a highly skilled technician. When this individual is absent, the optometrist fills in himself and takes fewer clients. Very small businesses like this one do face special challenges since an inevitable effect of their size is that very few coworkers are available to cover the work when someone is absent.

In virtually all the establishments we visited, managers had crafted solutions of one sort or another to the problem of covering the work of absent employees. Most were able to do so with little difficulty, although sometimes the costs in premium overtime pay or fees to temp agencies were significant. However, having contingency plans in place for such events is a business necessity, entirely apart from the question of family leave. Managers constantly face the possibility that an employee may quit precipitously, become seriously ill and unable to work, go on a military leave, take an extended vacation or unpaid leave, and so forth. Under all these circumstances, many of which occur on a regular basis, the work of absent employees must be covered. As a result, virtually all employers have established mechanisms for ensuring that work will be performed during employee absences—mechanisms they can deploy when employees take leave to care for a new child or seriously ill family member, just as for other absences.

Costs and Benefits to Employers of PFL

Prior to 2004, business groups raised the specter of huge hidden costs for employers if California implemented its PFL program—costs that, they claimed, could cripple California businesses and force them to lay off workers or move out of state. Our data show that this fear was unwarranted. Asked if the introduction of the PFL program had resulted in "any cost increases," 87 percent of respondents to our 2010 employer survey indicated that it had not. Some employers (9% of those responding to this question) indicated that the PFL program had generated cost *savings* for their organizations, by reducing employee turnover, reducing their own benefit costs, or both, when employees used the program instead of (or in combination with) employer-provided paid vacation, sick leave, or disability benefits.

Those employers who cover the work of employees on leave by assigning it to coworkers—which as we just saw is by far the most common approach—incur minimal extra costs as a result of any additional leaves that have resulted from the passage of PFL. Those who replace leave-takers with temps or by assigning overtime do incur some extra costs, even subtracting the savings from not paying the wages that employees on leave would have earned had they remained on the job. Indeed, among the 13 percent of respondents to the 2010 employer survey who indicated that PFL had generated cost increases, most reported additional hiring and training expenses to cover the work of employees who were out on leave. But for most employers these costs tend to be modest.

On the other hand, many of the employers who had provided their own paid leave benefits to employees prior to the creation of the state PFL program are now enjoying cost savings. Among employers responding to the

2010 survey, 60 percent reported that they coordinated their own benefits for exempt employees with PFL, and nearly as many (58%) did so for non-exempt employees. Similarly, about a third of the twenty employers we visited in our 2010 fieldwork coordinate company benefits with the state PFL program (A', B, H/I, N', and O) and realized a cost saving in that way, as table 4.9 shows. Case B requires employees to use the state program while the others strongly encourage its use. About 40 percent of these employers reported that they allow employees to use accumulated paid vacation or other paid time off at their discretion to top off the state benefit or to extend their leaves (cases C, D', J, K, M, P, and Q'). A few employers told us that their employees are more likely to use company-provided benefits than PFL (cases F, L, and P). Surprisingly, however, one company

TABLE 4.9.   Case studies, coordination of employer-provided benefits and PFL, California, 2010

Case code	Type of business	Total employees	Coordination of employer-provided benefits with PFL
A'	Manufacturing	4,894	HR encourages everyone eligible to use the program as that is a cost saving. Older workers often prefer to use accumulated sick leave and vacation pay to avoid PFL paperwork. But parents, who are younger and have had time to plan leaves during the pregnancy, typically use PFL, topping it off with sick leave and vacation pay.
B	Software design	2,781	The weeklong waiting period is fully paid by the company, and then the company coordinates with PFL benefits. Birth mothers on PFL can use vacation pay and/or up to 6 weeks of sabbatical pay if eligible. For fathers, company provides a one-week parental leave at 100% pay, and an additional 3 weeks leave coordinated with PFL.
C	Hospital	11,284	PFL is topped off from any available extended sick leave or paid-time-off benefits employee has accumulated.
D'	Computer engineering	20,000	Does not actively coordinate benefits with PFL, but company benefits can be used to extend leaves. Exempts have unlimited paid sick days; nonexempts must document time they are out of the office.
E	Optometrist	4	No coordination of benefits.

(Continued)

TABLE 4.9. *(Continued)*

Case code	Type of business	Total employees	Coordination of employer-provided benefits with PFL
F	Entertainment	1,300	No coordination of benefits. Most people (especially men) prefer to draw on accumulated vacation pay rather than PFL.
G	Food–headquarters	1,334	Employees who take PFL are placed on "no pay status" and may not coordinate PFL with accrued paid leave; but company does coordinate its benefits with SDI, which yields cost savings.
H/I	Food–processing and agricultural work	1,000	PFL is coordinated with company benefits for those who are eligible for the latter (only one segment of the workforce).
J	Insurance	2,000	Employees may draw on accumulated paid time off at their discretion to top off PFL. No direct savings for employer.
K	Apparel retail chain	561	Full-time employees, both exempt and nonexempt, can top off PFL with accumulated paid time off. No direct savings for employer.
L	Computer chip design	10,552	Company's own family leave program is easier to access than state program, take-up is low, no coordination of benefits.
M	Restaurant chain	630	Hourly employees may use any accrued paid vacation to top off PFL. No savings for employer.
N'	Life sciences/ biotechnology	108	PFL is coordinated with company benefits.
O	Law firm	270	For nonexempt employees company tops off PFL benefits so workers get up to 100% of pay (% depends on years of service). For lawyers, primary caregivers get 100% pay for the 6 weeks of PFL; secondary caregivers get 2 weeks.
P	Construction/ engineering	810	No coordination. Senior employees who have accumulated a lot of paid time off typically use that and don't bother with PFL.
Q'	Payroll processing	500	For minor (i.e., brief) leaves HR has some discretion and sometimes just lets exempts use sick leave for the whole period to avoid the paperwork hassles. For longer family leaves, California PFL can be concurrent with a vacation, and vacation leave can be used to top off.

Case code	Type of business	Total employees	Coordination of employer-provided benefits with PFL
R	Nonprofit research firm	819	There is no company-provided PFL program, but a payroll service provider administers the program and helps employees fill out forms. Some "whining" from non-California employees who don't have PFL. Providing the same company benefits across states is a problem even in regard to who to include. Company allows employees to take time off to care for a domestic partner, which was a contentious issue in their more conservative Arlington, Virginia, office.
S	Public utility	19,000	N/A
T'	Public-sector hospital	8,756	N/A

(case G)—a corporate headquarters—explicitly prohibits employees from drawing on paid vacation or other paid time off while using PFL.

Turnover and Retention

Turnover can be quite costly to employers. Replacing a worker who quits typically requires advertising the position and may also involve agency fees and candidate travel for interviews. A large company with high turnover may need to hire a staff of professional recruiters. As candidates apply for the position, employees must spend time reviewing resumes, carrying out preliminary telephone interviews, interviewing top candidates, calling references and doing background checks, and carrying out drug tests or physicals if required for the job. Once hired, a new employee's information must be entered into the payroll system and the employee enrolled in health insurance and other benefits. Often there is an orientation for new employees on "company time." And it takes time—from a few days to a few months, depending on the job—for a new employee to become fully productive. These are among the costs an organization may experience when it fills a vacancy. Insofar as PFL reduces turnover, then, employers may reap considerable savings.

In our 2004 employer survey, we collected data on the costs organizations incurred when filling a vacant position. To calculate the costs for filling a vacant nonexempt position (typically an hourly paid position) we collected information on (1) time spent by exempt employees screening applicants and doing paperwork; (2) agency fees, advertising costs, and related expenses; (3) training time for new nonexempt employees; and (4) average time for the nonexempt employee to achieve full proficiency. We made the simplifying assumption that proficiency increases in equal increments, so that a worker achieves 10 percent proficiency in 10 percent of the time it takes to achieve 100 percent proficiency. In this case, the employee's proficiency is 50 percent, on average, over the time period to achieve full proficiency. The employer, however, is paying full wages over this period. Thus, half the earnings of a new employee over the period when they are learning the job are a cost to the employer of filling the position. We multiplied time spent by exempt and nonexempt employees in these activities by the average wage of exempts and nonexempts respectively in the organization. We added these costs to find the total cost of replacing a nonexempt employee. We did the same calculation for exempt employees. Those costs varied with establishment size, as table 4.10 shows. Turnover costs for nonexempt workers varied from $4,149 (in 2009 dollars) to almost $8,043 in the largest organizations, while for exempt workers the range was from $12,625 to $18,331.[10]

TABLE 4.10.   Turnover costs for employers by firm size (in 2009 dollars)

	Nonexempt			Exempt		
	N	Average cost ($)	Average wage ($)	N	Average cost ($)	Average wage ($)
Firm size < 50	89	5,394	15.24	51	12,625	27.47
Firm size 50–499	58	4,149	12.03	49	13,912	21.70
Firm size 500+	51	8,043	17.95	48	18,331	29.92
Total	198	5,328	15.02	148	12,887	27.02

Source: Computed from authors' 2004 employer survey.

Calculating the annual earnings of employees in each category and comparing this with the cost of turnover, we found that it cost employers between 17 percent and 21 percent of the employee's annual salary to replace a nonexempt worker who leaves her or his job, and between 22 percent and 31 percent of the employee's annual salary to replace an exempt employee. On average, it costs 17 percent of annual salary to replace a nonexempt employee and 23 percent to replace an exempt employee. As these figures make clear, turnover is quite costly to employers, and retention can provide organizations with significant savings.

The overwhelming majority of employers (93%), as figure 4.3 shows, reported that California's PFL program had no effect or a positive effect in reducing turnover. Data from our 2009–10 employee survey shed additional light on this issue (see discussion in chapter 5). Among respondents to that survey who used PFL when they took a family leave, 83 percent returned at the end of their leaves to the same employer they had worked for previously compared with 74 percent of those who did not use PFL, although this difference was not statistically significant. California's PFL program may contribute to reduced turnover and thus provide another form of savings to employers. This is especially valuable for smaller employers that may be unable to afford high levels of wage replacement for workers who need to take a family leave but wish to retain those workers.

Conclusion

Despite widespread fears expressed by opponents of the program that PFL would create a heavy burden on the state's employers, our data suggest that they have had little or no difficulty adjusting to it. Five and a half years after PFL began operations, the vast majority of employers reported no effects or positive effects on their productivity or profitability (or, in the case of non-profit organizations, on their performance). Predictions that small businesses would find PFL especially burdensome were not borne out; on the contrary, among the few employers that did report negative effects, large businesses predominated. Cases of PFL abuse have also been rare, contrary to some predictions.

For many employers, PFL has been a source of cost savings, either due to reduced turnover or because they coordinated their own benefits with the state PFL program. Most employers reported that they covered the work of those out on leave by reassigning it to other employees, at little or no cost. A few employers did report higher costs due to the need to hire temporary replacements for employees on family leave, or for overtime pay. To the extent that the PFL program reduced turnover, however, the cost savings from improved retention helps to balance these additional costs.

5

The Reproduction of Inequality

Policies are not the same as *outcomes*. California's paid family leave program illustrates that truism all too well. The program was intended to function as a social leveler, with the key objective of ensuring universal access to partial wage replacement for baby bonding and caregiving leaves for all workers in California—including those whose employers provided minimal paid-time-off benefits or none at all. But nearly a decade after the program began operating, that outcome remains a distant goal. Many eligible workers do not even know that PFL exists, and even among those who are aware of it, take-up of the benefit has been limited. Moreover, those who are most in need of PFL—low-wage workers, young workers, immigrants, and disadvantaged racial and ethnic minorities—are especially unlikely to be aware of the program. These inequalities in awareness are all the more poignant in light of the fact that, for those who have taken advantage of it, PFL has been highly beneficial both economically and in terms of health outcomes, for both workers and their families.

This chapter draws on data from several surveys that we conducted between 2003 and 2011. In addition to the employer surveys discussed in chapter 4, selected data from which appear in this chapter, we focus on two other data sets. One is composed of a series of four surveys (partially described in chapter 3) that we designed to gauge public awareness of PFL among California adults. The other data set is made up of two detailed screening surveys of potential PFL recipients: the first was fielded in 2004, just before the program began operating, and the second in 2009–10, several years after PFL benefits became available. Both the four awareness surveys and the two screening surveys were conducted by telephone in both English and Spanish. (For more details on methodology, see the appendix.) But whereas the awareness surveys sampled the overall population of adult Californians, the screening surveys were designed to capture a sample of employed adults who had experienced a recent event (becoming a parent or having a close family member become seriously ill) that made them eligible for the PFL program. Although the screening surveys were not designed to be representative of the larger state population, focusing instead on individuals who were eligible for PFL benefits, the final samples (each of which included five hundred respondents) were demographically diverse in regard to age, gender, race and ethnicity, and immigrant status, and included workers across the economic spectrum, with varied levels of education and income.

As we documented in this book's introduction, inequalities between "haves" and "have-nots" in the United States have grown steadily in recent decades. The expanding ranks of low-wage workers who lack employer-provided health insurance coverage and other benefits present a stark contrast to professional and managerial workers who not only are paid relatively well but also typically have access to an array of employer-provided benefits. More specifically, this growing polarization among workers is manifested in the distribution of employer-provided wage replacement that can be used to support family leaves—ranging from paid sick leave and paid vacation to short-term disability benefits and paid parental leave—all of which are offered disproportionately to well-paid workers such as managers and professionals, while most low-wage workers have few or no such benefits.

As figure 5.1 shows, using data from our 2010 employer survey, larger employers and those with highly paid workers are far more likely than smaller employers and those with lower pay rates to provide their employees with paid sick days and paid vacation, both of which can serve as wage replacement during family-related leaves. This reflects the fact that employers tend to be especially interested in retaining their most highly trained workers, and they well know that providing such benefits increases retention.[1] By contrast, employers often consider low-wage workers dispensable and easily replaced and thus tend to be less concerned with reducing their turnover rates. As we showed in chapter 4, however, this view is problematic. Turnover costs tend to be substantial even in the case of hourly employees, varying from about $4,000 to $8,000 per employee.

To facilitate analysis of the variability in access to and use of paid leave, we divided the respondents to our 2009–10 screening survey into two key subgroups: those who held what we call "high-quality jobs," defined as jobs that pay more than $20 an hour *and* that include employer-paid health insurance, and those with "low-quality jobs" that fail to meet this standard. In our sample, 30 percent (149) of the respondents held high-quality jobs and 70 percent (351) held low-quality jobs—roughly similar to the proportions in other studies of California workers that differentiate between good and bad jobs.[2] Nearly all (94%) of the respondents to the 2009–10 screening survey with high-quality jobs had access to some

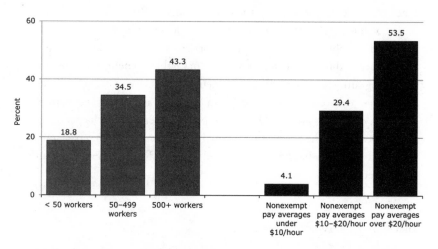

Figure 5.1. Percentage of establishments that offer paid sick days and paid vacation days to all non-exempt employees, by establishment size and average nonexempt pay, California, 2010. N = 253 for number of workers; N = 190 for average nonexempt pay. Authors' 2010 Employer Survey.

employer-provided paid sick days or paid vacation, or both, but only 62 percent of those with low-quality jobs had such access, a statistically significant difference.[3]

We exploit this division of the sample extensively below, comparing outcomes for these two groups when they experienced events triggering eligibility for PFL. This approach yields a variety of insights into the on-the-ground impact of the California program, and allows us to assess PFL's effectiveness as a social leveler in particular. From the outset, the potential impact was very different for the two groups: for professionals and managers and others in high-quality jobs whose employers previously provided them with access to some type of paid time off, the PFL program supplemented the benefits they already had, which were often as good or better than those now provided by the state. By contrast, low-wage workers who previously had limited or no access to wage replacement during leaves stood to gain far more from the new PFL program.

As we show below, those low-wage workers who have taken advantage of PFL have indeed benefited greatly from the new program, both economically and in terms of its impact on their health and well-being, as well as that of their family members. The program's potential to reduce inequality, however, remains largely unfulfilled. One reason for this is that many Californians remain unaware of the PFL program's existence. Another factor limiting the effectiveness of PFL as a social leveler is that it operates as a subsidy to those employers who have historically provided benefits of their own for workers who go on family leaves. A majority of those employers now coordinate their benefits with the state PFL program (see chapter 4), giving them an incentive to encourage their employees to access the state program. In contrast, low-wage workers who lack employer-provided benefits typically receive no such encouragement. As a result, the preexisting inequality in access to wage replacement during family leave has been reproduced in a new form, rather than being eliminated.

Inequality in Awareness of PFL

Over the past decade, we conducted a series of four surveys to assess the extent of public awareness of the program in California. The first such survey was fielded in the autumn of 2003, a year after the PFL legislation was passed (but prior to the program's implementation). At that time we found that only 22 percent of California adult respondents were aware of PFL. Awareness rose somewhat after benefits became available: our mid-2005 follow-up survey of California adults found that 30 percent of respondents were aware of the program a year after full implementation, and about the same proportion, 28 percent of respondents, were aware of it in mid-2007 when we conducted a third awareness survey (the difference between the 2005 and 2007 figures is not statistically significant). All three of these surveys, which used identical methodologies, found that low-income respondents, those with less education, young workers, Latinos, and immigrants had substantially lower levels of awareness of PFL than the state's adult population as a whole (not shown here, but see Milkman and Appelbaum 2004).

In 2011, in association with the California Field Poll, we once again assessed Californians' awareness of the state's PFL program. Although the methodology of the Field Poll was different from that used in the earlier awareness surveys in that it was limited to registered voters, the sample size was similar: it included 1,001 registered voters interviewed from September 1 to September 12, 2011. Well under half (43%) of the Field Poll respondents had "seen, read or heard" of the PFL program. As in the earlier surveys, awareness varied widely by gender, age, race and ethnicity, as well as education, household income, homeownership, marital status, between union and nonunion households, and by region, as figure 5.2 shows.

Female respondents were more aware of the program than males, which is not surprising given that women still are the primary caregivers in most families; in addition, women who draw on State Disability Insurance during their pregnancies receive a letter from EDD informing them about their eligibility for PFL. Respondents to the 2011 Field Poll aged 18–29, the prime childbearing ages (especially for less educated workers), were less aware of PFL than their older counterparts. Latinos and African Americans were also less aware than whites, although the difference was statistically significant only for Latinos. There was a direct relationship between household income and awareness, with low-income respondents significantly less aware of PFL than their more affluent counterparts. Reflecting similar economic disparities, renters were

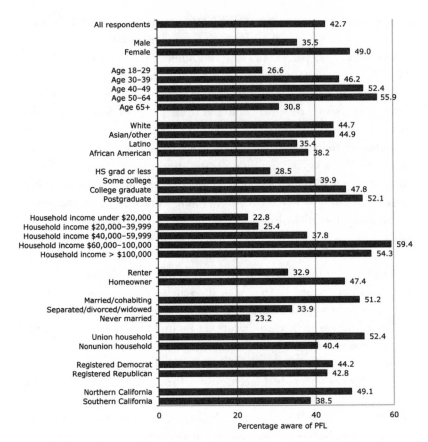

Figure 5.2. Awareness of paid family leave among registered voters in California, by selected respondent characteristics, September 2011. N = 1000. The categories Asian/Other, Whites, and Blacks do not include Latinos. For these race/ethnicity groups, using Whites as the reference group, the only statistically significant difference is for Latinos (p < .05). The gender differences shown are statistically significant (p < .001). Using age 40–49 as the reference group, the only statistically significant differences are for ages 18–20 and 65+ (for both p < .001). For household income, the differences between the top two and bottom two categories and the reference group (the middle category, $40,000–$59,999) are statistically significant (p < .05). For education, with college graduates as the reference group, the only statistically significant difference is for the high school graduates (which includes respondents with less than high school education), p < .001. The difference between renters and homeowners is also statistically significant, p < .001. Authors' analysis of 2011 Field Poll data.

less aware of PFL than homeowners, and married or cohabiting respondents were more aware than separated, divorced, widowed, and never married respondents. Those from union households were more aware of PFL than those with no union member in the household.[4] Finally, awareness was lower in Southern California than in Northern California, reflecting the higher concentration of Latinos and low-wage workers in the Southland.

Although the Field Poll sample, unlike that of the earlier awareness surveys, was limited to registered voters, we were able to systematically compare the 2011 data to the initial 2003 survey, which included questions about respondents' voting behavior. However, this comparison is limited to respondents who voted in the last general election (the 2008 election for the 2011 poll, and the 2000 election for the 2003 survey), so the data *do not* correspond to those shown in figure 5.2. As table 5.1 reveals, among those respondents who voted in the last general election, awareness increased by about 50 percent over the years between the first and the last surveys. Although fewer than half of these voters (45%) were aware of PFL in 2011, this was a dramatic and statistically significant increase over 2003, when the figure was only 30 percent. Awareness grew even more among female voters, from 26 percent to 51 percent, although for men there was little change. Moreover, awareness nearly doubled among Latinos and Asians who voted in the 2008 election. (However, this does not include the large population of immigrant noncitizens of all races and ethnicities, a disproportionately Latino group, because they were not eligible to vote and thus excluded from both the 2011 sample and from the 2003 subsample shown in table 5.1.)

The 2003 and 2011 awareness surveys did not probe in any detail the extent to which respondents were familiar with the details of the PFL program, nor how they learned about it. We were able to include questions about those topics in the 2009–10 screening survey, however. Not surprisingly, because all five hundred screening survey respondents were employed and all had experienced a life event (a new child or a seriously ill family member) that the PFL program was designed to cover, their awareness of PFL was somewhat greater than in the representative surveys, with nearly half (48.6%) indicating that they were aware of PFL's existence.

TABLE 5.1. PFL awareness among respondents who voted in the previous general election, 2003 and 2011 (%)

	2003	2011
All respondents	29.7	44.9*
Women	25.9	51.2*
Men	34.3	37.7
Latinos	22.0	40.8*
Blacks	35.3	38.0
Whites	30.9	45.7*
Asians/Other	24.9	49.3*

Source: Authors' analysis of 2011 Field Poll data (N = 1,000).
*p < .001 (comparing awareness levels in 2003 and 2011 for each group shown).

Among PFL-aware respondents to the screening survey, however, knowledge of the details of the program followed a similar pattern of inequality to that of the overall awareness data, as table 5.2 shows.[5] Respondents with high-quality jobs consistently knew more about the details of

TABLE 5.2. Knowledge of PFL program details by job quality, among respondents aware of PFL, 2009–10

	Percentage of PFL-aware respondents who knew specifics		
Specific information about paid family leave	All respondents	Respondents with high-quality jobs	Respondents with low-quality jobs
Can be used for bonding with a newborn	86.4	92.3	82.9*
Can be used for bonding with an adopted or foster child	68.5	75.9	63.6*
Available to both fathers and mothers	78.2	88.1	72.2***
Can be used to care for a seriously ill family member	64.2	68.2	62.0

Source: Authors' 2009–10 Employee Survey.
N = 246.
*p <.05; *** p < .001, comparing respondents in high- and low-quality jobs on each item.

the PFL program than those with low-quality jobs. Although these differences are more modest than those in overall awareness, all but one of them is statistically significant.

The 2009–10 screening survey also explored how PFL-aware respondents had learned about the program. As figure 5.3 shows, the most common source of information was employers: 63 percent of respondents employed in the private or nonprofit sector indicated that they had learned about the program from their employer—twice the proportion for any other information source except family or friends. Of particular interest for our purposes here, 78 percent of respondents in high-quality jobs had learned about PFL from their employers, compared to only 57 percent of those in low-quality jobs, a statistically significant difference.

This disparity reflects the reality, as noted above, that employers who provide paid time off to their workers have an economic incentive to inform those employees about the existence of PFL: if such workers draw benefits from the state PFL program in lieu of some part of what the employer would otherwise provide, the employer enjoys a cost savings. Since employers are more likely to provide wage replacement to

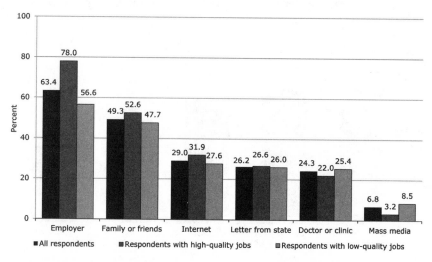

Figure 5.3. How respondents learned about paid family leave, California, 2009–10. N = 178. Includes only respondents who were PFL-aware and who were employed in the private or nonprofit sectors; total adds to more than 100% because respondents could cite more than one information source. Authors' 2009–10 Employee Survey.

higher-paid workers, it follows that those workers are more likely to receive information about PFL from their employers. As one manager we interviewed just before PFL benefits became available predicted, "Paid family leave in California was intended to help people who don't have any pay during maternity leave or other family leaves. But in fact the main beneficiaries will be higher-paid workers who already have paid sick leave and vacation and who will use the state program to top off their current benefits." Indeed, among PFL-aware respondents to our 2009–10 screening survey, half (50%) of those with high-quality jobs who were eligible for the program had used PFL, but only 37 percent of those in low-quality jobs had done so, a statistically significant difference.[6]

Limited awareness has also contributed to what has thus far been a lower-than-expected take-up rate for California's PFL program. The 2009–10 screening survey suggests some additional factors that help explain the low take-up rate. Among respondents who were aware of PFL, some were ineligible because they worked in the public sector, others were eligible but believed that they were not, and still another group received full pay from their employer while on family leave and thus had no reason to draw on PFL benefits. But even after eliminating all these groups from

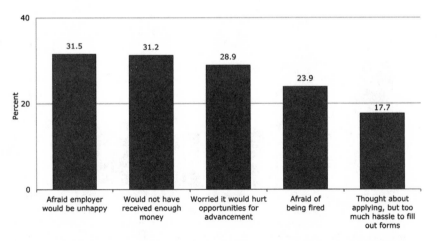

Figure 5.4. Reasons cited by selected PFL-aware respondents who did not apply for paid family leave, California, 2009–10. N = 89. Total adds to more than 100% because respondents could cite more than one reason. Authors' 2009–10 Employee Survey.

consideration, about a fifth of the total screening survey sample (those who were aware of PFL, worked in the private or nonprofit sector, believed they were eligible for the program, and did not receive full wage replacement from employer-provided sources while on leave) still did not use the PFL program for a covered life event. When asked why they did not apply for PFL when they needed to go on a family leave, these respondents cited a variety of concerns, listed in figure 5.4.

Caution should be used in interpreting these data, as the sample is limited and unrepresentative. Nevertheless, it is striking that many of the reasons cited involve concerns that taking advantage of PFL would have negative consequences for them at work: that their employer would be unhappy, that using PFL might hurt their chances for advancement, or, at the extreme, that they might actually be fired for doing so. In all, 37 percent of the subset of respondents who were asked why they did not apply for PFL cited at least one such concern.

This highlights a key limitation of the PFL program mentioned earlier in this book, namely, that it does not include job protection. Some PFL-covered workers do have job protection under the federal FMLA or the state CFRA statutes. But, for the rest, taking a PFL leave could mean that they would not have a job to return to, or that they would suffer other negative consequences. Fear of these outcomes appears to be a very important reason—second only to lack of awareness of the PFL program—for the low take-up rate. Finally, almost a third of the PFL-aware respondents who were asked why they did not use the program pointed to the limited wage replacement it provides, namely 55 percent of a worker's usual pay (and subject to income tax), which for many—especially those in low-wage jobs—may make it unaffordable.

The Impact of PFL on Low-Wage Workers and Their Families

For those workers who did use PFL, however, the program made a highly positive contribution to their well-being and that of their families. Respondents to the 2009–10 screening survey who utilized the PFL program when they took a leave from work to bond with a new child or to care for a seriously ill family member reported far better economic, social, and health-related outcomes than those who did not use the program. PFL users had significantly higher levels of wage replacement, were able to take longer leaves, and were more satisfied with the length of their leaves. Using PFL also enhanced workers' ability to care for their children or ill family members and, for those in low-quality jobs, increased the likelihood of returning to work with the same employer.

As we have seen, workers in low-quality jobs had the most to gain from the introduction of PFL, but they were less likely to be aware of its existence and (among those who were aware of it) less well informed about the details of the program than workers in high-quality jobs. But for the minority of workers in low-quality jobs who were not only aware of PFL but who actually used it during their family leaves, outcomes were greatly improved over those of workers in low-quality jobs who did not use PFL.

Wage Replacement during Family Leave

Most important, use of PFL made a significant difference in the level of wage replacement. Over one-fourth (28.4%) of all workers who did not use the PFL program during their leave, as table 5.3 shows, received no wage replacement at all. In contrast, the vast majority (92%) of those who used PFL while on leave received at least half their usual weekly pay, a far higher proportion (and a statistically significant difference) than among those who did not use PFL (59%).[7]

All workers who used the program benefited from PFL in regard to wage replacement, whether they were in high-quality or low-quality jobs. Among respondents with high-quality jobs, all of those (100%) who used PFL drew at least half their usual pay while on leave, compared to only 77 percent of those in high-quality jobs who did not use the program, a statistically significant difference.[8] However, many workers in high-quality jobs can draw on accumulated paid sick days, paid vacation, or other paid leave benefits for wage replacement when they go on leave. Indeed, in our sample, half (exactly 50%) of those in high-quality jobs who did not use PFL nevertheless received full pay from such sources. These employees, with access to generous employer-provided benefits, may not need PFL. But for all other respondents employed in high-quality jobs (i.e., those who

TABLE 5.3. Wage replacement during family leave, by PFL use and job quality, 2009–10 (%)

Proportion of usual pay received during leave	All workers			High-quality jobs		Low-quality jobs	
	All	Used PFL	Did not use PFL	Used PFL	Did not use PFL	Used PFL	Did not use PFL
No pay	21.8	0.0	28.4***	0.0	11.0*	0.0	38.2***
Less than half	11.5	8.3	12.5	0.0	12.4**	16.2	12.5
About half	20.1	40.2	14.1***	55.3	9.6***	25.9	16.7
More than half	20.0	43.1	13.1***	37.8	17.0	48.2	10.9***
Full pay	26.5	8.3	31.9***	6.9	50.0***	9.7	21.6
	100.0	100.0	100.0	100.0	100.0	100.0	100.0

Source: Authors' 2009–10 Employee Survey.
N = 204; columns may not add to 100% due to rounding.
*p < .05; **p < .01; ***p < .001, comparing respondents who used PFL and those who did not use it.

did not receive full pay), PFL sharply boosted the level of wage replacement, as table 5.3 and figure 5.5 show.

Workers in low-quality jobs received even greater economic benefits from PFL. Among respondents in this group who did not use PFL, 51 percent received either no wage replacement at all or less than half

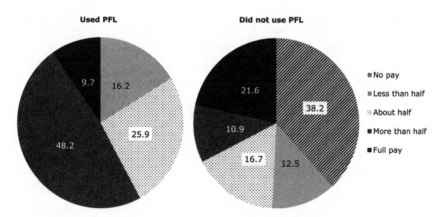

Figure 5.5. Wage replacement during family leave for workers in low-quality jobs, by PFL use, California, 2009–2010. N = 204. Authors' 2009–10 Employee Survey.

their usual pay. In sharp contrast, among those in low-quality jobs who used PFL, only 16 percent received less than half their income, a statistically significant difference.[9] All the other respondents in low-quality jobs who used PFL (84%) received at least half of their usual income while on leave, compared with only 49 percent of those who did not use PFL; this is a statistically significant difference.[10] For those low-wage workers who use it, then, the PFL program is a critically important source of income support when they go on leave from work to attend to their families' needs.

Public-Sector Workers and Wage Replacement during Leave

Most of California's public employees are not covered by SDI or PFL. Some public-sector employers have chosen to provide SDI and PFL coverage, which is optional for them (but legally required in the private sector), and in some cases public-sector unions have bargained successfully to obtain access for their members to the SDI and PFL programs (see Fendel et al. 2003). But, overall, less than one-fifth of the state's two million public-sector employees are covered by SDI and PFL.[11]

Although one might expect that public employees already have relatively high pay and benefits, and thus have little need for SDI or PFL, data from our 2009–10 screening survey suggest otherwise. As table 5.4

TABLE 5.4. Wage replacement during family leave, by sector and job quality, 2009–10 (%)

Proportion of usual pay received during leave	All respondents	High-quality jobs		Low-quality jobs	
		Public sector	Private/ nonprofit sector	Public sector	Private/ nonprofit sector
No pay	21.8	11.6	6.1	38.9	26.8
Less than half	11.5	14.6	6.1	9.9	14.6
About half	20.1	14.6	27.6	9.9	21.8
More than half	20.0	21.4	24.4	7.4	22.2
Full pay	26.5	37.8	35.7	33.9	14.6
	100.0	100.0	100.0	100.0	100.0

Source: Authors' 2009–10 Employee Survey.
N = 160; columns may not add to 100% due to rounding.

shows, many public-sector workers receive no wage replacement what-soever when they go on a family leave. This was the case for 12 percent of public-sector workers in high-quality jobs and for 39 percent of those in low-quality jobs. In our sample, workers in low-quality jobs had broadly similar patterns of wage replacement, regardless of whether they were employed in the public or private-nonprofit sector; indeed, a higher percentage of those in the public sector received 100 percent of their usual pay while on family leave. Among those in high-quality jobs, however, more than half as many public-sector as private/nonprofit sector workers received less than half their usual pay, or no pay whatsoever, while on family leave. However, these differences are not statistically significant.

Length of Leaves

Although PFL made a substantial difference in access to wage replace-ment during leave, especially for those in low-quality jobs, its effects on the length of family leaves were more complex. As table 5.5 shows, the median

TABLE 5.5.   Median length of family leave (in weeks), by gender, leave type, and job quality, 2009–10.

	All respondents	**High-quality jobs**		**Low-quality jobs**	
		Male	**Female**	**Male**	**Female**
All respondents who used family leave					
Baby bonding leaves	9.5	3	14.5***	3	12***
Ill family member caring leaves	4	3	3.5	6	8
Used paid family leave					
Baby bonding leaves	12.5	4	18*	8	12
Ill family member caring leaves	7	3	5	6	11
Did not use paid family leave					
Baby bonding leaves	8	2	12***	3	12***
Ill family member caring leaves	4	3	3	4.5	8

Source: Authors' 2009–10 Employee Survey.
N = 98 for bonding leaves, N = 53 for caring leaves. *p < .05; *** p < .001 using the Mann-Whitney-Wilcoxon test to compare reported leave lengths by gender.

length of baby bonding leaves taken by all new parents in our sample was 9.5 weeks. Mothers took longer bonding leaves than fathers, regardless of job quality, and in most subgroups these gender differences were statistically significant (the one exception was for those in low-quality jobs who used PFL). However, for leaves to care for an ill family member, there was no significant gender difference in median leave length.

Among mothers in low-quality jobs, the median length of leave was the same whether they used PFL or not. Mothers in high-quality jobs took longer bonding leaves, however, with a median length of eighteen weeks for those who used PFL, compared to only twelve weeks for those who did not take advantage of the program.[12] This may reflect the fact that many employers coordinated their own paid leave benefits with the state PFL program.

As figure 5.6 shows, most respondents (79%) reported that they were "very satisfied" or "somewhat satisfied" with the length of their family leaves. Among workers in high-quality jobs, many of whom had access to income from employer benefits while on leave, satisfaction

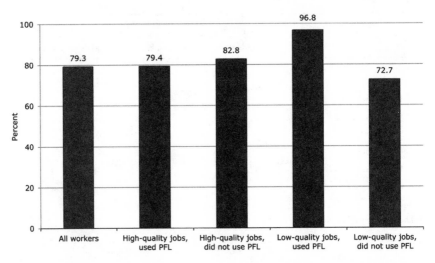

Figure 5.6. Percentage of workers who were "very satisfied" or "somewhat satisfied" with length of family leave, by job quality and use of PFL, California, 2009. N = 164. Authors' 2009–10 Employee Survey.

with the length of leave was similar regardless of whether they used PFL or not: about four-fifths of these workers reported that they were very satisfied or somewhat satisfied with the length of their leave. For workers in low-quality jobs, however, the use of PFL made a striking difference in satisfaction with the length of leave. Among workers in these jobs, nearly all (97%) of those who used PFL were very satisfied or somewhat satisfied with the length of their leave, compared with only 73 percent of those who did not use PFL, a statistically significant difference.[13]

Turnover and Retention

Nearly all (95%) respondents to the 2009–10 screening survey who took a family leave returned to work afterward, and more than four-fifths of them returned to the same employer they had worked for prior to the leave. As figure 5.7 shows, the proportion of workers returning to the same employer was highest among respondents in high-quality jobs who did not use PFL. This may be due to the more generous employer-provided pay

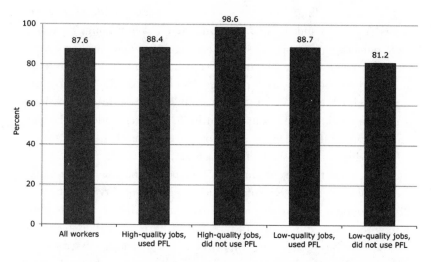

Figure 5.7. Percentage of workers who returned to former employer after a family leave, by job quality and use of PFL, California, 2009–2010. N = 165. Authors' 2009–10 Employee Survey.

these workers received during leave—as noted above, nearly half the respondents in high-quality jobs who did not use PFL received full pay from their employers.

Among workers in low-quality jobs, however, use of the PFL program is associated with a slightly greater likelihood of returning to the same employer after a family leave. Within this group the retention rate was 89 percent for those who used the PFL program compared with 81 percent for those who did not. Although the difference is not statistically significant, it nevertheless suggests the possibility that California's PFL program may provide an important benefit for employers of low-wage workers, especially smaller employers who are unable to afford high levels of wage replacement for workers on family leave but who do wish to retain those workers.

PFL's Effects on Caregivers and on Those Receiving Care

The screening survey also documents the impact of PFL on outcomes for care recipients and caregivers, including the effects on the ill family member's health, the ability of respondents to care for new children and for seriously ill family members, new mothers' ability to initiate and to sustain breastfeeding, and parents' ability to make childcare arrangements. Table 5.6 and figure 5.8 summarize our key findings regarding these outcomes. As table 5.6 shows, among respondents in low-quality jobs, 87 percent of those who used PFL reported that the leave positively affected their ability to care for the new child, compared with 72 percent of those who did not use PFL, a statistically significant difference. Moreover, as figure 5.8 shows, about four-fifths (82%) of respondents who took leaves reported that the leave had a positive effect on their ability to care for their child or seriously ill family member.

Most new mothers in our sample (85%) reported that they had breastfed their babies. Nearly all (94%) of new mothers in low-quality jobs who used PFL had initiated breastfeeding, and the rate was nearly as high (89%) among those who did not use PFL. Although PFL use had no impact on the duration of breastfeeding for workers in low-quality jobs, for those in high-quality jobs the duration of breastfeeding among those who used PFL was more than double that of those who did not use it (a statistically

TABLE 5.6.   Family leave effects on caregiving ability and health of care recipients, by job quality and use of PFL, 2009–10

Effects of leave	All respondents	High-quality jobs		Low-quality jobs	
		Used PFL	Did not use PFL	Used PFL	Did not use PFL
Percent who state that leave had positive effect on ability to care for new child or ill family member (N = 164)	82.3	100.0	91.8*	87.0	72.2*
Percent of new mothers who initiated breastfeed-ing (N = 67)	91.3	88.5	89.7	89.1	94.0
Median months of breastfeeding (N = 57)	6	11.5	4.5**	4.5	5
Percent who state that leave had positive effect on ability to arrange childcare (N = 92)	62.5	56.7	67.4	70.0	58.3
Percent who state that leave had positive effect on ill family member's health (N = 49)	86.5	100.0	100.0	69.2	79.9

Source: Authors' 2009–10 Employee Survey.
Note: For median months of breastfeeding, the Mann-Whitney-Wilcoxon test was used.
*p < .05; **p < .01

significant difference). Previous research suggests that longer leaves for new mothers are associated with longer duration of breastfeeding (Calnen 2007; Guendelman et al. 2009); our results offer some confirmation of this but also suggest that there may be important variation by social class (see Blum 2000).

Leaves were also helpful in enabling parents of a new child to make childcare arrangements. Among all parents, 63 percent reported that PFL had a positive effect on their ability to arrange childcare. Among parents in low-quality jobs, 70 percent of PFL users reported a positive effect, compared to 58 percent who did not use PFL; however, this difference is not statistically significant.

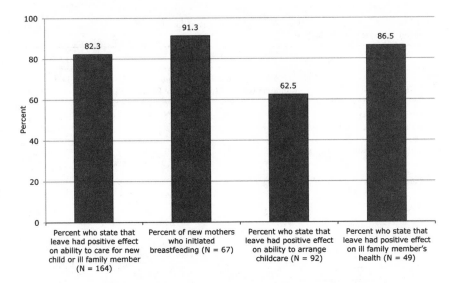

Figure 5.8. Effects of PFL use on employee outcomes, California, 2009–10. For median months of breastfeeding, the Mann-Whitney-Wilcoxon test was used. Authors' 2009–10 Employee Survey.

Conclusion

In some respects, California's PFL program provides a pathbreaking and positive model—one that might be replicated by policymakers in other states and nationally. Our findings suggest that public policy initiatives that support workers who need time off to care for their families can make a real and positive difference. Although by international standards California's PFL program offers minimal benefits, it has led to substantially improved economic, social, and health outcomes for the workers who have taken advantage of it, and better outcomes for their families as well. As we have shown, wage replacement levels were significantly higher for workers who used PFL than for those who did not, especially for workers in low-quality jobs. Moreover, workers in low-quality jobs who used PFL were more likely than those who did not use the program to return to the same employer after a family leave, were more satisfied with the length of their leave, were better able to care for newborns and ill family members, and were better able to make childcare arrangements.

At the same time, however, California's experience with PFL offers a cautionary tale about the key obstacles such programs must overcome. These obstacles are different from those so often highlighted by business spokespersons who routinely oppose the efforts of advocates to create new programs to address work-family needs. The persistence of unequal access to paid time off even after the implementation of PFL is the single most serious problem. Not only is general public awareness of the PFL program woefully limited, as we have seen, but those who stand to benefit most from it are the least likely to be aware of it. Low-wage workers, Latinos, Blacks, and young workers have especially low awareness levels regarding the program—the very groups that have limited access to other sources of wage replacement during family leaves.

The main source of information about PFL, for those workers who are aware of it, is employers. Whereas employers who previously provided some form of paid time off to workers and now coordinate those benefits with the state program stand to gain if employees use the state program, those who provide no company-paid benefits have little incentive to inform employees of the program. This, along with unequal awareness, has generated a dynamic that re-creates the previous inequality in access to wage replacement during leaves in a new form.

There are other challenges as well. Even among workers who were aware of PFL, as we have seen, some did not apply for the program when they needed a family leave because the wage replacement level was too low. Many of them feared that taking PFL would lead to negative consequences for them on the job, perhaps even leading them to be fired. The lack of job protection in the PFL program is a serious concern for many workers.

In short, the potential of California's new program to extend access to paid leave to all the state's workers, including those who previously lacked access to wage replacement, has yet to be fulfilled. Until awareness of PFL spreads more widely, especially among low-wage workers and other disadvantaged groups, and until the issues of job protection and more extensive levels of wage protection are addressed, the program will not achieve its intended effect of reducing the long-standing disparity between workers—most of them well-paid managers and professionals— who previously had access to paid leave via employer-provided benefits and the less-privileged workers who lacked such access.

We do not wish to suggest that the PFL program does not have important benefits for workers in better-quality jobs. On the contrary, the fact that PFL directly benefits both higher-strata workers and California employers themselves (who bear no direct costs for it) is a crucial feature of the program's political viability and sustainability. The challenge that remains, however, is to ensure that PFL benefits are universally accessible in practice as well as in theory. We explore the policy implications of our findings further in the next chapter.

6

Conclusions and Future Challenges

Changing family and work patterns in the United States—increased maternal labor force participation, the aging of the population and the accompanying growth in the need for eldercare, along with rising male participation in parenting and family caregiving—have dramatically expanded demand for paid family leave. Apart from the business community, which consistently opposes public policy initiatives that address this issue, there is a broad public consensus in support of paid time off for workers when they have new children or need to care for seriously ill family members. Politically, this issue transcends the usual Left-Right divisions, as we saw in chapter 2. Liberals support paid leave as part of the government's obligation to provide an economic safety net for working families, while conservatives endorse it as a form of state support for "family values." As a result, as various polls and surveys show, paid leave has broad support across the political spectrum and among all demographic groups: large majorities of men and women, rich and poor, immigrants and those born in the United States, and people of all races and ethnicities approve of paid family leave programs like the one California created in 2002.

The positive effects of access to PFL for workers are widely recognized in previous literature. The incidence and length of breastfeeding, so vital to the health of both mother and infant, increase when a new mother can take paid time off from work to bond with the baby. Adults as well as children recover from serious illness more quickly when cared for by a family member, which is more feasible when paid leave is available. PFL also contributes to narrowing gender inequalities: not only does fathers' involvement with newborns increase when they have access to paid leave, but among women who can take paid time off to deal with family care responsibilities employment stability is enhanced; as a result, paid leave reduces the wage penalties typically associated with motherhood.

Not surprisingly, our data on California confirm these findings. As we showed in chapter 5, PFL use is associated with better economic, social, and health outcomes for workers and their families. Wage replacement levels were higher for workers who used PFL than for those who did not, especially among those in low-quality jobs (defined here as jobs that either pay $20 or less per hour or do not offer access to employer-provided health insurance). Workers in low-quality jobs who used PFL were more likely than those who did not use it to return to the same employer after a family leave, were more satisfied with the length of their leaves, were better able to care for newborns, and were better able to make childcare arrangements. California's PFL program also had positive effects on workers in high-quality jobs, for example in increasing breastfeeding duration.

Beyond contributing additional evidence documenting the positive effects of paid leave, our study of California's decade-old PFL program has led us to advance three new arguments in this book. The first involves the *politics* of winning programs like the one in California. As we showed in chapter 2, the vast breadth of public support for PFL means that the inevitable business opposition to legislative initiatives creating paid leave programs can be neutralized with effective coalition building, at least in states and localities where key elected officials (governors, mayors, and key legislative leaders) are not irrevocably opposed to them.

Coalitions including organized labor, senior citizens' organizations, women's groups, and advocates for public health and for children won PFL in California and a similar program in New Jersey. Laws guaranteeing paid sick days have also been passed in several jurisdictions through such coalition efforts.

It is our hope that this approach will eventually secure PFL legislation at the federal level as well. Our research suggests that attempts to appease business by proposing minimalist legislation or by carving out exemptions in response to business pressure will prove futile; the historical record shows that business lobbyists can be counted on to oppose even the most moderate regulations or mandates, even worker-financed paid leave insurance programs like those in California and New Jersey. Their opposition is rooted in ideological opposition to governmental intervention in the workplace, and to the market fundamentalism that is so politically influential today. The challenge is to isolate business lobbyists and employer associations politically by building an effective coalition in support of paid leave legislation, a coalition composed of the many groups (including some businesses) that support the idea. Making "the business case" for paid leave can help neutralize the effect of business lobbying against it, but no amount of negotiation will lead Chambers of Commerce to abandon their opposition.

That said, the second key argument of this book contributes greatly to the "business case" in illuminating the basic *economic* dynamics of paid leave. In chapter 4, we showed that even though employers overwhelmingly opposed PFL, in fact it has very few negative effects on them and in many cases actually offers substantial economic benefits. Our surveys and interviews with California employers themselves, conducted more than five years after PFL was implemented in that state, offer definitive evidence that the new PFL program was a "nonevent" for the vast majority of businesses. Our data reveal that employers themselves report that PFL had no effect or a positive effect on the productivity, profitability or performance, turnover, and worker morale of their organizations. Moreover, many employers enjoyed cost savings as a result of the program, and abuse was rare.

Our third argument is more sobering. Despite its many benefits for workers and their families that we and others have documented, the California PFL program has not yet fulfilled its promise as a social leveler. Most well-paid professionals and managers already had access to employer-provided paid-time-off benefits as good as or better than those the state program now provides before it became law; thus workers in low-quality jobs were those who stood to gain the most from PFL. But as we showed in chapter 5, the fact that awareness of the program's existence remains limited, especially among those who are in most need of paid leave—low-wage workers, young workers, members of disadvantaged racial and ethnic groups, and immigrants—means that it has not fulfilled its potential to narrow class disparities in access to paid leave. Instead, the preexisting inequality in access has been reproduced to an extent that urgently deserves further attention from policymakers. Moreover, our survey data suggest that, even among those who are aware of PFL, fear of negative on-the-job consequences has led many Californians not to take advantage of the program. And others who are aware of PFL have declined to use it due to the limited amount of wage replacement it provides. All these findings have implications for future policymakers crafting paid leave programs for other states and nationally.

Lessons from California's PFL Experience

We surveyed a representative sample of California employers in 2004, just before the program was implemented, and again in 2010, after PFL had been operating for over five years. If employers were experiencing serious problems as a result of the program's implementation, this surely would have been apparent by the time of the 2010 survey. But such problems proved to be few and far between, just as was the case after the federal Family and Medical Leave Act (FMLA) became law in 1993, again despite strong business opposition. As previous studies document and our own 2004 data confirmed, conforming to the requirements of FMLA had little to no impact on employers' profitability or performance, and often improved morale and reduced turnover. But FMLA leaves were unpaid; arguably paid leaves could be different. As we have seen, business groups were adamantly opposed to the PFL legislation, and some politicians as well as members of the public were persuaded by their claims that it would be unduly burdensome, especially for small businesses. There was widespread recognition of workers' need for paid time off to care for new children and ill family members, but in the absence of solid evidence about the effects of programs like California's PFL on businesses, it was difficult to counter the claims of state Chambers of Commerce and other employer lobbyists that the program would be a "job killer" and impose crushing costs on employers.

Workplace Flexibility 2010 at Georgetown University Law School, a national initiative that aimed to develop consensus around the need for flexible work arrangements and paid time off, offers an illustration of this challenge. It brought together representatives of employers, labor, work-family advocates, and researchers in a sustained dialogue over a period of years to explore potential public policy solutions to employees' work-life dilemmas with the goal of enhancing flexibility in the workplace. This effort succeeded in forging a broad consensus on flexible work arrangements but, according to the conveners, the group could not achieve similar agreement on paid leave. "Everyone acknowledged there was a problem: People need paid time off for their own health and family caregiving and lots of people, across incomes and industries, don't get it," they reported. "But we simply couldn't come up with an alignment of interests between employers and employees about the role of government and public policy in this equation. Workers' need for time-off policies is deep, but the concerns of employers are deep as well: How would public policy intersect with how they do business?" (Workplace Flexibility 2010 and CHEFS 2010, 5).

Our data on California's program directly answer this question about the intersection of business and public policy, demonstrating that the fears expressed by opponents of PFL that it would be unacceptably burdensome on the state's employers have not been borne out. Instead, employers themselves reported that they have had little difficulty adjusting to it. As detailed in chapter 4, five and a half years after PFL began operations the vast majority of employers we surveyed reported positive effects or no effect on their productivity or profitability (or, in the case of non-profit organizations, on their performance). Similarly, predictions that small businesses would find it especially difficult to adapt to PFL proved unfounded; on the contrary, among the few employers that did report negative effects, large businesses predominated. Cases of PFL abuse—another concern raised by opponents of the California legislation—were also rare: the vast majority of employers knew of no cases of abuse.

For many employers, rather than adding a cost burden, PFL gener-ated cost savings, because they coordinated their own wage replacement benefits (such as paid sick days or vacation, or in a few cases paid pa-rental leave) with the state-sponsored PFL program, or because of the ways in which PFL use reduced turnover, or both. A few employers did report higher costs due to the need to hire temporary replacements for workers who took family leave, or to pay overtime premiums to the coworkers who assumed the duties of leave-takers. But most employers covered the work of those out on leave by reassigning it to other em-ployees, at little or no cost. Moreover, as we documented in chapter 4, virtually all organizations have long-standing contingency plans—many of them quite creative—to cover the work of absent employees, since at any time workers may quit without warning, become seriously ill, or even die unexpectedly. The need for such contingency plans, indeed, long predated PFL.

This is not the only reason that the California law had little or no ef-fect on most employers' business operations. Another is that while wel-coming a new child into a family or coping with the serious illness of a spouse, parent, or other close relative is a major life event for the worker involved, such situations typically affect only a small percentage of the labor force in any given year. When family emergencies do arise, most households today have no one at home available to address them, since every available adult is already in the workforce. For that reason, with or without access to PFL or its equivalent, many employees take time off after the birth of a child or when serious illness strikes a family member.

Although business arguments against PFL and similar policy proposals often claim that such programs are especially burdensome for small busi-nesses, our findings suggest precisely the opposite. Many large employers already provide paid vacation and sick leave benefits that can be cobbled together by employees to provide income when they need a family leave. Small employers often regret that they lack the resources to provide simi-lar benefits to their valued employees. This may even place some of them at a disadvantage compared to larger companies in recruiting top talent. California's PFL program helps solve this problem, with no direct costs to the small businesses involved.

Future Challenges for California's PFL Program

Despite the many positive achievements of California's pioneering PFL program, serious challenges remain. As we documented in chapter 5, awareness of the program remains unacceptably low, especially among those who need paid leave most: low-wage workers, young workers, Latinos, Blacks, and immigrants. When PFL was created, many hoped it would reduce the preexisting inequality in access to wage replacement during family leaves; indeed, for those low-wage and other disadvantaged workers who are aware of the program and its provisions, this hope has been realized. Unfortunately, however, both general public awareness of PFL and awareness among those who stand to benefit most from it are woefully limited. The main conduit of information about the program to eligible workers is employers—especially those who have long provided some type of paid-time-off benefits themselves and who now coordinate those benefits with the state PFL program. The result is that the previous pattern of inequality in access to paid leave has been reproduced in a new form.

Our analysis suggests the following specific recommendations for improving California's existing PFL program:

Expand outreach. It is crucial to expand outreach and education efforts that specifically target the groups that have the least awareness of the program: low-wage workers, young workers, immigrants, and members of disadvantaged minority communities. One approach in regard to bonding leaves might be to require hospitals to inform all new parents of the availability of PFL, a standard practice in Australia since its new paid leave program began operating in 2011 (resulting in far higher awareness rates than in California). More generally, hospitals, doctors, and health clinics should be required to make PFL brochures and application forms available in their offices and facilities. California's Women, Infants and Children Supplemental Nutrition agencies should be required to do the same.

Provide job protection. Fear of retribution, as we have seen, prevents many workers from using PFL even when they are aware of it. Job protection (which guarantees the right to return to the same or a comparable job) should be extended to cover everyone who is eligible for a PFL leave, not just those who already have such protection under other laws. No one should be forced to risk their job to attend to a new baby or meet other vital family needs.

Increase the level of wage replacement. The PFL program currently provides 55 percent of weekly earnings; this is inadequate for many workers and dissuades many of those who need leave from taking up PFL. The benefit should be increased to at least 75 percent of usual weekly earnings to make taking PFL affordable to more workers. This could be done with a negligible increase in the payroll tax funding the program benefit.

Extend PFL to cover all California public employees. At present, most public-sector workers are not eligible for PFL or SDI. As we saw in chapter 5, this is highly problematic for many public-sector workers, especially those in low-quality jobs. Like their private-sector counterparts, these workers should have access to wage replacement when they need to take family leave.

Designing a National Paid Leave Program

As has often been the case in the history of the United States, state-level initiatives can serve as valuable testing grounds for the development of national policies that enhance public welfare. Indeed, the California PFL experience documented in this book offers some valuable lessons for the design of a national insurance program to provide universal access to paid leave. Also relevant is the experience of California and several other states with paid temporary disability insurance for workers whose own serious health problems or pregnancies temporarily prevent them from working; these TDI programs have existed for over six decades. In both respects the nation's most populous state's history of social provision offers several lessons for national policymakers:

No carve outs. California's experience shows that paid leave can be extended to virtually all employees, including low-wage workers and those employed part-time, without significant disruptions to business operations. Although the overwhelming majority of California employers reported no impact or a positive impact of PFL, small employers had even more positive outcomes than larger businesses. Paid leave should be available to all workers, regardless of the size of their employer. As in the California program, previous work and earnings requirements should be modest, so that low-wage and part-time workers who contribute to paying for the program are eligible to receive its benefits.

Payroll tax a non-issue. Economists have long recognized the distinction between the legal incidence and the economic incidence of a tax. Regardless of whether a program like PFL is paid for through a tax on employers or one on employees, it is the supply of and the demand for different types of labor that determines who actually bears the tax burden. When a high-tech employer transfers a systems analyst from a facility in Austin, Texas, to one in Silicon Valley, the employer increases that worker's wages to cover California's higher payroll taxes. The law imposes those taxes on workers, but in this instance it is the employer who actually pays it, albeit indirectly. Conversely, in the case of workers whose skills are in abundant supply, a payroll tax charged to employers will ultimately be passed on to workers by means of offering new hires a lower starting wage and providing incumbent employees with reduced pay increases.

In both California and New Jersey, the law imposes the taxes financing PFL entirely on employees. Although on the surface this may appear unfair, in fact it is a reasonable and effective approach. The payroll tax is modest, the benefits of the program are highly valued by employees, and they cannot buy this insurance for themselves in the open market. It is neither realistic nor wise to require all employers to provide PFL benefits directly (although some may do so voluntarily to retain especially valued employees or those with firm-specific skills); since the cost of paid leave varies with the age and gender composition of the workforce, such a mandate could put some employers at a competitive market disadvantage. The government-administered insurance programs pioneered by California and New Jersey avoid this problem entirely.

A broad wage base. Tax rates are lower when the wage base for the tax is broader. New Jersey uses the unemployment insurance wage base ($30,300 a year) in setting the tax rate for its family leave insurance program. That is, the tax is paid on only the first $30,300 of income. California uses a much broader tax base ($95,585 a year) for its PFL program. The Social Security wage base, currently $110,100, is broader than either of these, and easy to administer since it is already widely used. In California, the combined tax rate for both SDI and PFL is a low 1.0 percent; it would be even lower if it were based on the Social Security wage base.

A separate trust fund for national paid family leave in Social Security. Long before legislating their PFL programs, both California and New Jersey had TDI programs in place, and in both states PFL is administered as a separate trust fund within the preexisting state agency that had managed TDI for decades. This greatly facilitated implementation of the family leave programs, as we saw in chapter 3, and has kept administrative costs low. Our survey respondents who used the PFL program found it easy to utilize, reported that their applications were processed efficiently, and that their payments were received promptly.

The existence of separate trust funds for TDI and PFL protects the integrity of both programs. At the national level, the prime candidate for the location of a separate trust fund for PFL is the Social Security Administration (see Boushey 2010; Boushey and Glynn 2012). The use of such an existing administrative structure would make it possible to quickly implement a new program, and a separate trust fund for PFL would protect the integrity of Social Security's traditional programs.

Allow employers to "top off" the state benefit if they so wish. In California, employers who already had generous paid leave policies were able to realize cost savings by coordinating company-paid benefits with the state program. Thus many companies who had formerly paid workers' full salaries during a family leave now encourage or require them to collect the first 55 percent of wages from the PFL program and then "top off" the state benefit by paying the remaining 45 percent. In New Jersey, employers' initial fears that workers would double dip—collecting full pay from employers while also drawing on the state benefit—were later allayed and workers in this state are also able to receive payment from both sources while on family leave. The result is that New Jersey employers are able to realize the same cost savings that their California counterparts enjoy by coordinating benefits.

Broad and inclusive definition of family. Blended families, extended families, and other nontraditional families all rely at one time or another on employed family members for care when they are seriously ill. A national paid leave program should respect the diversity among contemporary families and encompass a highly inclusive definition of "family member." In addition to the spouses, children, parents, and registered domestic partners covered by California's PFL program, paid leave should be available to care for siblings, grandchildren, and grandparents, at least.

Job protection. Fear of retribution from employers—losing opportunities for advancement or promotion, or even being fired—is one reason that many workers who are eligible for California's PFL program choose not to take advantage of it. A national paid leave program should make it illegal to fire workers or to discriminate against them in other ways if they take up family leave.

Equal access to paid leave for men and women. Male and female workers in California have equal access to PFL to bond with a new child or to care for a seriously ill family member. This should be a feature of any national program as well. As we saw in chapter 3, men in California have substantially increased their use of PFL for bonding leaves since the inception of the program, and employers report that new fathers have been taking more and longer leaves than they did before the program existed. By increasing male participation in parenting in this way, PFL can help reduce gender inequality in both the household and the labor market.

In short, a national paid leave program that would enable all workers to take the time they need to bond with a new child, care for a seriously ill family member, or recover from their own illness without being forced to choose between meeting these basic human needs and the economic well-being of their families, is not only desirable but also feasible. That is the positive lesson of California's experience with paid family leave. At the same time, it is critical that such a program be truly universal in its scope, with extensive public outreach to ensure that all those who need it are aware that it exists and can easily access the benefits. Paid family leave is available in every other advanced nation in the world, and it already has strong support across the U.S. political spectrum. Addressing this part of the nation's unfinished business should be an urgent priority.

METHODOLOGICAL APPENDIX

This book includes analysis of original survey data that we collected from employers and workers in California before and after the state's paid family leave program went into effect. First, we systematically surveyed over 250 employers and five hundred workers in the state in the first half of 2004, just before PFL payments began (on July 1 of that year), providing detailed baseline data on how the types of life events for which benefits would soon become available under the new PFL program—becoming a parent or needing to care for a seriously ill family member—were being handled in the absence of the program. We went on to conduct a second round of surveys of employers and workers several years after the program had begun operating, in late 2009 and early 2010, which provide a richly detailed portrait of the impact of PFL on employers and workers that we draw on throughout this book.

This was never meant to be a longitudinal study; all four surveys were cross-sectional. However, our original hope was that the "before" and "after" surveys would enable us to systematically compare things such as the frequency and length of family leaves taken by workers, or the extent to which employers provided their own wage replacement benefits, before and after PFL benefits were available. However, that turned out to be far more difficult than we had anticipated. The Great Recession that began in late 2007, which had a severe impact on California, made direct comparisons between our 2004 and 2009–10 data extremely problematic. Unemployment remained abnormally high at the time of the follow-up surveys; even among workers who were employed, insecurity and fear of job loss was far more widespread than in 2004. Many employers were also deeply affected by the recession, especially smaller employers. All this as well as some other unforeseen methodological challenges (described below) made it impossible to carry out the "before" and "after" comparisons we originally envisioned. Nevertheless, the four surveys offer a great deal of valuable data about employers' and workers' experience with California's landmark PFL program.

Employer Surveys

We surveyed 263 California employers by telephone during the period from March 8 to May 21, 2004, to learn how they were handling the kinds of family leaves for which the state PFL program—already created by law but not yet fully implemented—would soon cover. The University of California at Berkeley's Survey Research Center (SRC) fielded the survey on our behalf. Almost six years later, from January 13 to May 18, 2010, we did a second telephone survey of 253 establishments. It was fielded for us by the Center for Survey Research at the University of Massachusetts, Boston. (By that time the SRC had ceased to exist due to budget cuts.) Although the 2010 survey replicated many aspects of the 2004 survey, there were some important differences between their sampling frames and weighting methodologies.

Sampling

Both the 2004 and 2010 employers were designed with stratified samples of California worksites drawn from the Dun and Bradstreet (D&B) database. In both surveys, establishments with varying numbers of employees were sampled at different rates. Since there are many more small than large establishments in the state of California (and therefore in the D&B database), this strategy was used to increase the number of large establishments in the final sample, allowing us to compare small and large businesses systematically.

The sampling frame for the 2004 employer survey was derived in part from a survey the SRC had conducted the previous year, the *Survey of California Establishments* (SCE). Although it focused primarily on other issues, at our request that survey included a few questions about paid family leave (some of the results are reported in chapter 2 of this book; additional results and the SCE methodology are described in Milkman and Appelbaum 2004). The SCE sample was drawn from the D&B database of California establishments with at least one employee. Government agencies, public schools and universities, as well as agriculture, forestry, and fishing establishments were excluded from the sample, which was stratified into seven size categories: 5–9, 10–19, 20–49, 50–99, 100–249, 250–999, and 1000+ employees. The strata were sampled at progressively higher rates, ranging from 0.97 percent for the category with the smallest establishments to 100 percent for the category with the largest establishments, with the aim of obtaining roughly equal numbers of respondents from each stratum. Establishments with fewer than five employees were excluded from the SCE sample.

Our 2004 employer survey on PFL leave also had a stratified sample design, but with fewer strata than the SCE. It included three of the original seven categories in the SCE: 5–24, 50–499, and 500+ employees. But since we were especially interested in the impact of PFL on small businesses, and firms with fewer than five employees had not been included in the SCE, we constructed a fourth stratum of establishments with 2–4 employees, drawing a new random sample of eligible establishments that size from the D&B database. For the three larger size categories (establishments with at least five employees), random samples were drawn from establishments that had been respondents to the previous SCE. This method produced relatively high response rates (which we later adjusted for in weighting the data, as discussed below) for those three categories, as table A1 shows.

The 2010 employer survey sample, unlike its 2004 counterpart, was freshly drawn from the D&B database of California worksites. As in 2004, government agencies, public schools and universities, and establishments

TABLE A1.   Raw response rates by
establishment size, 2004 employer survey

Establishment size	Raw response rate (%)
2–4 employees	30.8
5–49 employees	63.1
50–499 employees	50.4
500+ employees	61.0

in agriculture, forestry, and fishing were excluded. The goal was to construct a sample using the same establishment size categories (2–4, 5–49, 50–499, and 500+ employees) as in 2004, but because in 2010 all four strata were untested in previous surveys, the two samples are not directly comparable.

Another important modification in the sampling approach in the 2010 survey was introduced after data collection had already begun. Although the original design had called for completing 250 interviews with employers evenly distributed across the four strata, it quickly became apparent that the stratum with 2–4 employees was problematic to implement, due to the effects of the Great Recession. Although officially the recession was over well before early 2010, this period was a very difficult one for small employers in California such as those we were attempting to sample. Many businesses in the stratum with 2–4 employees listed in the D&B database had collapsed by the time of our 2010 survey. Phone numbers listed in the database were often out of service and new phone numbers could not be obtained; in other cases we were able to verify that the establishment was no longer in business or no longer had employees. Overall, only about 20 percent of sampled businesses in the 2–4 employee stratum were eligible for the survey, compared to 60 percent in the 5–49 employee stratum and over 80 percent in the two strata with largest establishment sizes. Another problem was that the number of employees listed in the D&B database was often higher than the number that establishments reported in the actual survey, because the recession had led many of them to downsize. To address these difficulties, we decided to merge the two smallest establishment size categories (2–4 employees and 5–49 employees) into one larger stratum in our analyses of the 2010 data.

Weighting and Response Rates

As shown in table A2, we used weights to adjust the response rates to the 2004 survey to take account of its reliance on the earlier SCE sample. The results shown are comparable to the AAPOR Response Rate 1. Table A2 also shows the distribution of the sample among the four strata in each of the two surveys. (The response rates shown in table A2 for the three largest strata in the 2004 survey differ from those shown in table A1 because they are weighted to control for the effects of reliance on the SCE and to make them comparable to the 2010 rates.)

The two employer surveys were analyzed with two distinct weights: "establishment weight" and "worker weight." Using the establishment weights yields results that consider all establishments equally, regardless of size; analysis using the worker weights yields results that adjust for the variation in establishment size and thus estimate the proportion of all workers affected by an employer policy or sharing an employer characteristic. The worker weights were created by multiplying the establishment weight for each case by the number of employees in the establishment (and then rescaling, as noted below).

Both these weights were also adjusted for nonresponse. For this purpose, the establishment weight for each case was divided by the response rate for its establishment size category (and then rescaled). The nonresponse-adjusted version of the worker weight was created by multiplying the number of employees by the nonresponse-adjusted

TABLE A2.   Adjusted response rates and sample sizes, 2004 and 2010 employer surveys

	2004 Survey		2010 Survey	
Establishment size	Adjusted response rate (%)	Sample N	Adjusted response rate (%)	Sample N
2–4 employees	30.8	69	22.7	17
5–49 employees	33.5	65	26.6	85
50–499 employees	25.5	65	27.1	84
500+ employees	24.5	64	19.9	67
Total	28.6	263	24.3	253

Note: Response rates shown assume that establishments of unknown eligibility were eligible for the survey.

version of the establishment weight. This procedure yields the weights we used in the text when estimating results for establishments across size categories.

Although the basic weighting approach was similar in both the 2004 and 2010 surveys, there are some differences, most of which derive from the differences in sampling described above. First, since the 2004 sample for the three larger employer size categories was drawn from the 2003 SCE, the weights used for analyzing it incorporated the establishment weights from that survey along with the other weights to produce estimates for the four establishment size strata. In contrast, since the 2010 survey sample was drawn directly from the D&B database, only one weight was used initially for each of the four strata. However, since in the 2010 survey the two smaller size categories were combined in the final analysis, two different weights were used for the 2–49 employee stratum for which results are reported in the text.

Second, the number of workers used to construct the worker weights differed between the two employer surveys. In the 2004 survey, the number of workers that each establishment reported in response to the survey itself was used for this purpose. In contrast, in the 2010 survey the count of workers used in constructing the worker weights was drawn from the D&B database (rather than from the survey itself). Finally, in the 2004 survey both the establishment and worker weights were scaled so that the weighted number of cases was equal to the number of observations in the sample. In contrast, the 2010 survey scaled the cases to equal the number of establishments and workers in the state of California.

Worker Surveys

The 2004 and 2009–10 worker surveys did not seek to obtain representative samples of the California workforce, but instead were designed from the outset as screening surveys that targeted workers who had experienced life events—adding a new child to their families or caring for a seriously ill family member—that would make them eligible for PFL. Both workers surveys used cross-sectional list-assisted random digit dialing (RDD) telephone samples covering all telephone exchanges in the state of California. In both years, English- and Spanish-speaking interviewers were available, so that monolingual Spanish speakers and Spanish speakers with limited English proficiency could be included. Both surveys had final sample sizes of five hundred.

In the first worker survey, five hundred California workers were interviewed by telephone from February 24 to June 2, 2004, about the ways in which they were handling the kinds of family leaves that the state PFL program—passed into law but not yet fully implemented—would soon cover. Like the 2004 employer survey, the 2004 worker survey was fielded by the SRC at the University of California at Berkeley. The second telephone worker survey of five hundred workers was conducted from December 3, 2009, to February 26, 2010, by the California Survey Research Services in Van Nuys, California. (As noted above, the SRC had ceased to exist due to budget cuts.) Although the 2010 survey replicated the 2004 survey in many respects, there were some important differences in the sampling methodologies each used.

In 2004, screening of potential respondents was based on two criteria. First, respondents had to be currently employed or actively seeking work, or to have been employed in the previous two years. (Self-employed individuals were excluded.) Second, to be eligible for the survey, respondents had to be part of a household in which an adult had primary responsibility for the care of a newborn, newly adopted child, or new foster child, or for the care of a seriously ill child, parent, spouse, or domestic partner; or in which an adult anticipated having such responsibilities in the next two years.

In 2009–10, similarly, respondents to the worker survey had to be currently employed or actively seeking work, or to have been employed in the previous two years. This survey also screened for an adult household member with primary responsibility for a new child or a seriously ill child, parent, spouse, or domestic partner over a four-year period; however, the time frame in 2009–10 was the four years prior to the survey interview (whereas in 2004 the period included two years prior to the survey interview as well as anticipated events in the following two years).

Another difference between the two surveys involved inclusion in 2009–10 of households whose only telephone was a mobile (cellular) phone. The number of such households had increased dramatically in the period since the 2004 survey, and such households are known to include a disproportionate number of younger respondents as well as those with lower incomes, both populations of interest to us. In addition, because RDD surveys generally had experienced declining response rates over time, in 2009–10 we offered incentives to respondents for participating in the survey. Those who completed interviews received a $20 gift card ($40 for the cell-phone-only cases) for use at a local supermarket. No such incentives were offered in the 2004 worker survey.

In both 2004 and 2010, the results reported in chapter 5 were weighted to adjust for the number of eligible persons in each household as well as for the number of telephones in each household. Both factors affect the probability of selection in any RDD survey. The fifty cell-phone-only household cases were also weighted to reflect the fact that in California an estimated 9 percent of households relied exclusively on cellular phones at the time the survey was conducted, according to the Centers for Disease Control and Prevention.

Response Rates

Tables A3 and A4 summarize the response rates for the two worker surveys. There were two key points when potential respondents could decline to participate in the study: when initially contacted but prior to being screened for eligibility, and after being screened but prior to consenting to the full interview. These two sets of refusals are shown separately in the tables below.

In 2004, almost one-third (30.6%) of successfully contacted households refused to participate at the screening stage. Among those who continued beyond that point, 15 percent met the screening criteria for the survey and were selected for interviewing; however, within this group about one-fourth (25.7%) of successfully screened, eligible respondents refused to participate at the next stage.

Table A4 presents the data separately for the 450 landline cases and the cell-only households in the case of the 2009–10 worker survey. As it shows, among the landline cases, response rates at the initial point of contact were far lower than in 2004: over two-thirds (69.1%) of successfully contacted households refused to participate prior to being screened for eligibility. Among those who continued beyond this point, 11 percent met the screening criteria for the survey and were selected for interviewing;

TABLE A3.   Response rates for 2004 worker survey

	Number	Percentage of total	Percentage of eligible households	Percentage of eligible respondents
Total selected phone numbers	8, 166	100.0		
No answer after at least 9 calls	927	11.4		
Ineligible: Not a household	3,354	28.8		
Ineligible: Not English/ Spanish speaking	115	1.4		
Other ineligibles	35	0.4		
Eligible for screening	4,735	58.0	100.0	
Screening nonresponse	1,462	17.9	30.9	
Successfully screened	3,273	40.1	69.1	
No responsibility for new child/ill family member	2,303	28.2	48.6	
Not employed or self-employed	262	3.2	5.5	
Total ineligible households	2,565	31.4	54.2	
Total eligible households	708	8.7	15.0	100.0
Later determined ineligible	35			4.9
Eligible for interview	673			95.1
Respondent refusals	154			22.9
Never home/unable to participate	19			2.8
Total nonresponse	173			25.7
Completed interviews	500			74.3

within this group of successfully screened and eligible respondents, about one-fifth (19.4%) refused to participate at this later point. Among the cell-phone-only households, over nine-tenths (91.3%) of successfully contacted households refused to participate prior to being screened for eligibility. Among the remaining households, 18 percent met the screening criteria for the survey and were selected for interviewing; within this group, however, one in six respondents refused to participate at the later stage.

TABLE A4. Response rates for 2009–10 worker survey

	Number	Percentage of total	Percentage of eligible households	Percentage of eligible respondents
Households with landlines				
Total selected phone umbers	39,054	100.0		
No answer after 7 calls	8,340	21.3		
Ineligible: not a household	13,598	34.8		
Ineligible: not English/ Spanish speaking	336	0.9		
Other ineligibles	99	0.3		
Eligible for screening	16,681	42.7	100.0	
Screening nonresponse	11,524	29.5	69.1	
Successfully screened	5,157	13.2	30.9	
No responsibility for new child/ill family member	4,181	10.7	25.1	
Not employed or self-employed	408	1.0	2.4	
Total ineligible households	4,589	11.8	27.5	
Total eligible households	568	1.5	3.4	
Eligible for interview	673			100.0
Respondent refusals	110			19.4
Never home/unable to participate	8			1.4
Total nonresponse	118			20.8
Completed interviews	450			79.2
Cell-phone-only households				
Total selected phone numbers	10.000	100.0		
No answer/voicemail (average of 3.3 attempts)	3,055	30.6		
Ineligible: not a household	2,733	27.3		
Ineligible: not English/ Spanish speaking	34	0.3		
Other ineligibles	476	4.8		
Eligible for screening	3,702	37.0	100.0	

	Number	Percentage of total	Percentage of eligible households	Percentage of eligible respondents
Screening nonresponse	3,373	33.7	91.1	
Successfully screened	329	3.3	8.9	
No responsibility for new child/ill family member	249	2.5	3.7	
Not employed or self-employed	20	0.2	0.3	
Total ineligible households	269	2.7	4.0	
Total eligible households	60	0.6	0.9	
Eligible for interview	60			100.0
Respondent refusals	10			16.7
Never home/unable to participate	0			–
Total nonresponse	10			16.7
Completed interviews	50			83.3

These low response rates are unfortunately typical of RDD surveys conducted in the early twenty-first century. Both the 2004 and 2009–10 screening survey samples, however, proved demographically diverse in regard to age, gender, race, ethnicity, immigration status, education, and income, like the California workforce from which they are drawn. Although not representative samples, they nevertheless offer many valuable insights regarding the impact of PFL on workers.

Notes

1. Introduction

1. Heymann and Earle (2010, 111) surveyed 190 countries and found that, among the 181 for which adequate data were available, only Swaziland, Papua New Guinea, Australia, and the United States lacked national policies guaranteeing paid leave for new mothers. Australia is no longer on the list, as it implemented a new paid family leave policy in 2011. See http://www.humanservices.gov.au/customer/services/centrelink/paid-parental-leave-scheme?utm_id=10.

2. FMLA also provides unpaid job-protected leaves to care for a seriously ill spouse, child, or parent, or for a worker's own serious illness.

3. Five states—California, Hawaii, New Jersey, New York, and Rhode Island—as well as the U.S. territory of Puerto Rico have temporary disability programs, which were created in the 1940s to cover temporary disabilities (other than those covered by workers' compensation) that required workers to be absent from work for an extended period. In the 1970s these programs were extended to cover pregnancy-related disability (see chapter 2 and Vogel 1993).

4. For more details on the New Jersey program, see White, Houser, and Nisbet 2013. Washington State passed paid family leave legislation in 2007, but to date the program remains unfunded and thus nonoperational. Several other states are considering similar legislation.

5. The ATUS found that women spent an average of 1.07 hours per day and men .43 hours per day performing physical care for children in households whose youngest child was under age six; for all forms of "caring for household children as a primary activity," women spent an average of 1.71 hours per day while men averaged .88 hours per day. These data are

averages for the combined years 2007–11. The ATUS found that female eldercare providers averaged .87 hours per day on eldercare in 2011, while their male counterparts averaged .57 hours per day. (These data include all caregivers, not only those who were employed.) See U.S. Department of Labor 2012a, tables 9 and 15 (ratios reported in the text were computed by the authors).

6. The gender gap in access to paid time off has narrowed since Heymann wrote this, however. The 2011 ATUS found that 58% of female wage and salary workers had access to some type of paid leave, only slightly below the 60% of male wage and salary workers who had such access (U.S. Department of Labor 2012b, table 1).

7. The distribution of paid vacation for state and local government workers (shown in table 1.1) is technically an exception to the regressive pattern characteristic of access to paid leave discussed in the text. This reflects the fact that elementary and secondary school teachers, who make up a large share of the upper quartiles of state and local government workers, rarely have paid vacation as a formal fringe benefit. Although they have a great deal of time off in the summers, it is not considered "vacation." Thanks to John Schmitt for pointing this out to us.

8. These data are for "single jobholders" only; that is, workers who held two or more jobs are not included.

9. The 2010 Affordable Care Act included an amendment to the Fair Labor Standards Act that now requires employers to provide break time and private space for new mothers to express breast milk for one year after a child's birth.

10. Notable exceptions include Heymann 2000; Albiston 2010; Gerstel and Armenia 2009; and Williams 2010.

11. The long hours demanded of those who aspire to successful careers in elite occupations in the United States present a sharp contrast with the European pattern. Richard Freeman (2007, chap. 4) has linked this to the relatively high level of inequality in the overall U.S. earnings distribution, arguing that the most elite U.S. workers receive disproportionately large returns for working extremely long hours.

12. Self-employed individuals may opt into both SDI and PFL. Public sector workers can also be covered if the agency or unit that employs them opts into the program; however, less than 20% of the state's public-sector workers are currently covered in this way (e-mail communication with the state Employment Development Department, November 15, 2010). For more details on eligibility, see chapter 3.

2. The Politics of Family Leave, Past and Present

1. For details on ongoing campaigns around the country, see the database maintained by the National Partnership for Women and Families, at http://www.nationalpartnership.org/site/PageServer?pagename=issues_work_database.

2. This modification was less problematic than the reduction in the maximum leave length, because, had it become law, most employers would have passed on the cost of the employer portion of the payroll tax to workers—in most cases by reducing (or not increasing) some other component of their overall wage and benefit package. More generally, the economic incidence of a tax (who actually pays for it) is often independent of its legal incidence (who the law levies the tax on). Some groups of workers—for example, union members or those whose skills are rare or highly valued by employers—may have enough bargaining power to prevent employers from passing on the costs of such a tax to them. But for low-wage workers, such as those who stood most to gain from California's PFL law, employers will shift most or all of the tax to workers either by offering slightly lower pay to new hires or by reducing pay increases for incumbent workers. In such cases, whether the tax is levied on workers or employers, workers will end up absorbing the cost.

3. Another nation Esping-Andersen lists in this category is Australia, which until recently was the world's only other economically advanced country (besides the United States) with no paid family leave program; however, Australia began operating such a program in 2011.

4. Dobbin, however, gives these female managers too much credit, in our view, going so far as to argue that "because personnel experts had already put maternity and medical leaves in place by 1993, the main effect of the law was to popularize formal employer leave policies for paternity and for care of sick family members." Coverage for the latter types of leaves (rarely available prior to the passage of the FMLA) did increase particularly sharply after 1993, but, as Waldfogel has shown, coverage for (unpaid) maternity leaves also increased dramatically just after FMLA became law, rising from 60% to 93% of medium and large companies between 1993 and 1997, and from 18% to 48% in small ones (fewer than one hundred employees) between 1992 and 1996 (Waldfogel 1999, 14) Dobbin also neglects the point we emphasized in chapter 1, that is, that employer-provided leaves are disproportionately offered to managers and professionals.

5. As Vogel (1993) elaborates, this question is linked to a larger theoretical debate among feminists about "difference" and "equality," which we do not take up here. See also Fraser 1994; Gornick and Meyers 2009.

6. The case that involved ectopic pregnancies was *Rentzer v. California Unemployment Insurance Appeals Board*, 32 Cal. App.3d 604, 108 Cal. Rptr. 336 (Cal. App.2.Dist. 1973). The Supreme Court case was *Geduldig v. Aiello*, 417 U.S. 484 94 S.Ct. 2585, 41 L. Ed. 256 1974.

7. The full name of the case is *California Federal Savings and Loan Association, et al., Petitioners v. Mark Guerra, Director, Department of Fair Employment and Housing et al.* 479 U.S. 272 (107 S.Ct. 683, 93 L.Ed.2d 613).

8. The text of the bill, which was approved by the governor on October 10, 1999, and its full legislative history, is available at http://legix.info/us-ca/measures;1999-00;sb0656/doc@96.

9. California's wage replacement rate (55%), however, is lower than that in Hawaii, New Jersey, and Puerto Rico. New Jersey, New York, and Puerto Rico's maximum benefit duration is twenty-six weeks, while in Hawaii and Rhode Island it is thirty weeks. For more details, see Workplace Flexibility 2010 and CHEFS 2010, 40.

10. A similar coalition—also with strong leadership from labor unions—underlay the passage of paid parental leave legislation in Australia in 2010. See Baird and Whitehouse 2012.

11. The rest of this section is based on Firestein and Dones 2007 and on Labor Project for Working Families 2003, unless otherwise indicated.

12. Some advocates feared that including domestic partners would become a political lighting rod, but Senator Kuehl, herself a lesbian, insisted on including this provision. This issue, as it turned out, was never raised by opponents of the PFL bill.

13. For the complete list, see Labor Project for Working Families 2003.

14. Orfalea is cited in Firestein and Dones 2007, 146; Hoffman is quoted in Jones 2002.

15. By contrast, immediately after the gubernatorial recall election, the "pay or play" health care legislation that the state legislature had passed earlier in 2003, after a hard-fought labor-led campaign, was reversed in a referendum campaign supported by Schwarzenegger and the Republican Party, as well as by employer and business interests.

3. Challenges of Legislative Implementation

1. The legislation requires employers to notify employees hired after January 1, 2004, and those who are taking a leave that they might be eligible for PFL benefits. They must also display a poster with information about PFL (along with information about SDI and unemployment insurance) in the worksite. Finally, employers who offer a private family leave plan in lieu

of the state PFL are required to demonstrate that their coverage exceeds that in the state plan (a similar requirement to that for employers who use private insurance in lieu of SDI, as noted in chapter 2).

2. The information in this paragraph and the preceding one is from field notes Ruth Milkman recorded at a Paid Family Leave symposium in Sacramento sponsored by EDD on December 1, 2009, entitled "The First Five Years," where administrators described the implementation process.

3. The 2003 survey and its methodology are described in more detail in Milkman and Appelbaum 2004. Our 2005 and 2007 follow-up surveys used the same methodology and had similar sample sizes. In all three surveys, respondents were asked the same question, except that in 2003 the wording indicated that the program would take effect the following year, and the dollar figure for the maximum benefit was updated each time. The 2007 version was: "Have you seen, read, or heard anything about a new California law that took effect in 2004, which provides up to 6 weeks of paid family leave for eligible workers at 55% of their weekly earnings, up to a maximum of $882 per week?"

4. In 2004, shortly before PFL benefit payouts began, the Chamber published an excellent guidebook, *Managing Leaves of Absence in California Made Easy*, which is the source of the information presented in this section, unless otherwise indicated.

5. Workers covered by FMLA/CFRA have had the right to continuing benefits since the early 1990s. In 2011 a new California law was passed requiring employers to continue health insurance benefits for all workers during PDL leaves. Prior to that employers were only required to do so for those not protected by FMLA/CFRA if it was their practice to maintain such benefits for other types of disability leaves.

6. Exceptions require employers to prove that no comparable position is available or that filling an available comparable position would undermine the business's ability to operate.

7. In those initial years, the polarization of PFL take-up by earnings bracket followed a similar pattern, but was less pronounced. See Sherriff 2007.

8. Unfortunately, the Employment Development Department was unable to provide us with more recent data on PFL take-up by establishment size.

9. The data in figure 3.2 are for fiscal years, which in California begin on July 1 of each calendar year.

4. Paid Family Leave and California Business

1. In fact a leave to care for "Aunt Mary," even if she were seriously ill, would not be eligible for PFL, since aunts are not among the family members the program's caregiving leaves cover (only seriously ill parents, children, spouses, and registered domestic partners of a covered worker are included in the program).

2. All results reported in this chapter are weighted (using the establishment weights described in the appendix) to adjust for the overrepresentation of large firms in the sample, and to adjust for nonresponse. The 2004 and 2010 samples were independent of one another; this was not a longitudinal study. For details on the survey methodology, see the appendix.

3. These interviews ranged from thirty minutes to two hours in length each, and at most worksites we interviewed at least two managers. This was a convenience sample. Because of the difficulties in gaining access to worksites, and the fact that "family friendly" employers tend to be more receptive to requests for interviews than other employers, the establishments we visited are not a representative sample of California employers (unlike the surveys). Rather the fieldwork was biased in favor of employers with a relatively high level of concern with work-family balance, most of whom offered unusually extensive family-leave-related benefits. Although a few small businesses are included, most of our cases are relatively

large establishments; in this respect as well they are not representative of the overall population of employers in the state. Indeed, as table 4.1 shows, all but one of the case study establishments we visited in 2004 were covered by the FMLA, which does not cover small employers. About a third of the employers we visited were members of the UCLA-based Human Resource Round Table who agreed to participate in the study as a result of a request from its director. Another set of site visits (about a fourth of the total) were arranged with members of One Small Step, a San Francisco Bay Area employer group focused on work-family issues. Access to the rest of the cases came through contacts from our personal networks. Only one of the many "cold calls" we attempted resulted in a successful interview. We added one more case in 2010, case T, a public-sector hospital that we had not visited in 2004. Cases H and I are divisions of a large food company, where we conducted separate interviews in 2004; in 2010 information on both divisions was provided by the same respondent. We also conducted similar fieldwork interviews in New Jersey prior to the introduction of paid family leave insurance there; our findings from that research are reported in Appelbaum and Milkman 2006.

4. Nonexempt employees are those covered by basic employment laws like the 1938 Fair Labor Standards Act, which established the minimum wage and the forty-hour work week as well as mandating extra pay for overtime hours. Many states have passed similar legislation setting higher standards than those required by federal law. Managers and some other upper-level employees are "exempt" from such laws, hence this terminology.

5. The Ns for figure 4.2 were 96 for the question on profitability, 95 for the questions on productivity and turnover, and 92 for the question about morale.

6. N = 169.

7. For nonprofits, which make up about one-fifth of the overall sample, the question was asked about "performance"; the rest were asked about "profitability."

8. Four of the twenty establishments did not have any experience with the PFL program. The public sector hospital (case T) is not covered by the PFL program at all (public-sector workers are not covered unless they actively opt-in through the collective bargaining process). Cases L, P, and S all chose to be self-insured, offering somewhat superior benefits to those in the state program.

9. Most of the differences shown in table 4.6 by establishment size were not statistically significant, with the following exceptions: small establishments were significantly different from medium and large ones in the frequency with which they assigned work to others ($p < 0.05$); small establishments were significantly different from medium ones in the frequency with which they put work on hold ($p < 0.001$); small establishments were significantly different from medium ones in the frequency with which they had workers do some work while on leave ($p < 0.05$); small establishments were significantly different from medium ones in the frequency with which they hired replacements ($p < 0.05$); medium establishments were significantly different from large ones in the frequency with which they hired replacements ($p < 0.001$); and small establishments were significantly different from medium ones in the frequency with which they reported using some other method to cover the work ($p < 0.05$). Note that the significance results denoted by asterisks in table 4.6 are not by firm size but rather for the comparisons between exempt and nonexempt workers.

10. Prior to computing these estimates, we imputed missing data for cases where information was missing on some elements needed to calculate the cost of turnover. Imputation was performed by first separating the data into three establishment-size strata (fewer than 50 employees, 50–499 employees, and 500+ employees), and then, within each stratum, imputing missing values as the median value for the variable. We used median values (rather than means) so that the final results would err on the conservative side and not be distorted by a few high values. The imputation process had a small effect on median turnover costs ($4,174 unimputed for nonexempts compared with $3,965 imputed; $12,578 unimputed for exempts compared with $12,794 imputed). We then calculated average cost of turnover for

exempt and nonexempt employees to facilitate comparison with the average annual earnings. We weighted average costs of turnover to account for overrepresentation of some firm sizes in the sample. Average turnover cost unimputed for nonexempts is $4,474 and for exempts is $11,834. The unimputed turnover cost for nonexempts is 14% of annual earnings; for exempts, it is 20% of annual earnings.

5. The Reproduction of Inequality

1. Note that whereas figure 4.1 shows the establishments that offered these benefits to *any* workers in 2004, figure 5.1 shows only those that offered these benefits to *all* nonexempt workers in 2010. The categories shown in each of these two figures differ in other details as well.

2. See, for example, Fligstein and Sharone's analysis of the California workforce in 2001–02, which found two worlds of work, one at the top "with lots of pressures but many rewards . . . in income . . . job satisfaction, paid benefits and more security on the job," comprised of 34% of the workforce; the other 66% had work that was "more onerous . . . with fewer paid benefits and . . . more insecurity" (Fligstein and Sharone 2002, 91–92). By the time we conducted our second screening survey in 2009–10, almost a decade later and immediately following the Great Recession, the proportion of desirable jobs was presumably slightly lower.

3. P < .001 using a two-sample independent Z-test. All significance levels reported are based on Z-tests, unless otherwise noted.

4. See Kramer 2008 regarding the ways in which unions raise awareness of FMLA; it seems likely that a similar dynamic is at work here.

5. Some of the findings from the 2009–10 screening survey reported in this chapter differ from those reported in Appelbaum and Milkman 2011, because we have corrected some errors in the analysis on which that earlier report was based.

6. P < .05. Eligible respondents are those employed in the private or nonprofit sectors (since most public-sector workers are not eligible for the state PFL program). Take-up rates did not vary much by race, ethnicity, or between U.S.-born and immigrant workers.

7. P < .001. This figure is not 100 percent because some respondents took leaves longer than the six weeks for which they could receive wage replacement through the state PFL program.

8. P < .001.

9. P < .001.

10. P < .001.

11. Unpublished data, Employment Development Department, State of California.

12. P < .01, using the Mann-Whitney-Wilcoxon test.

13. P < .001. The other differences in satisfaction levels shown in figure 5.6 are not statistically significant.

REFERENCES

Albiston, Catherine R. 2010. *Institutional Inequality and the Mobilization of the Family and Medical Leave Act: Rights on Leave*. New York: Cambridge University Press.

American Academy of Pediatrics, Committee on Hospital Care. 2003. "Family-Centered Care and the Pediatrician's Role." *Pediatrics* 112: 691–96.

Anderson, Hil. 2002. "Calif. Gov. Signs Family Leave Measure." United Press International, September 23.

Appelbaum, Eileen, and Ruth Milkman. 2006. *Achieving a Workable Balance: New Jersey Employers' Experiences Managing Employee Leaves and Turnover*. New Brunswick, N.J.: Center for Women and Work, Rutgers University.

——. 2011. *Leaves That Pay: Employer and Worker Experiences with Paid Family Leave in California*. Available at http://www.cepr.net/index.php/publications/reports/leaves-that-pay.

Baird, Marian, and Gillian Whitehouse. 2012. "The Australian Union Movement and Paid Parental Leave: Strategic Coalitions and Campaigns." Unpublished paper presented at the International Sociological Association Forum, Buenos Aires, Aug. 1–4. Copy in authors' possession.

Berger, Lawrence, Jennifer Hill, and Jane Waldfogel. 2005. "Maternity Leave, Early Maternal Employment, and Child Health and Development in the U.S." *Economic Journal* 115: F29–47.

Bernick, Michael. 2000. *The Fiscal Impact on the Disability Insurance Fund of Extending Disability Benefits to Individuals Granted Family Medical Leave*. June. Sacramento, Calif.: Employment Development Department.

Bernstein, Anya. 2001. *The Moderation Dilemma: Legislative Coalitions and the Politics of Family and Medical Leave*. Pittsburgh, Pa.: University of Pittsburgh Press.

Bianchi, Suzanne. 1995. "Changing Economic Roles of Women and Men." In *State of the Union: America in the 1990s*, edited by Reynolds Farley, vol. 1, 107–54. New York: Russell Sage Foundation.

Blair-Loy, Mary. 2003. *Competing Devotions: Career and Family among Women Executives*. Cambridge: Harvard University Press.

Blum, Linda M. 2000. *At the Breast: Ideologies of Breastfeeding and Motherhood in the Contemporary United States*. Boston: Beacon Press.

Boushey, Heather. 2010. *Social Security Cares*. Washington, D.C.: Center for American Progress.

Boushey, Heather, and Sarah Jane Glynn. 2012. *Comprehensive Paid Family and Medical Leave for Today's Families and Workplaces*. Washington, D.C.: Center for American Progress.

Bravo, Ellen. n.d. [ca. 1992]. "Wage Replacement for Family Leave: Is It Necessary? Is It Feasible?" Mimeo. Cleveland: 9to5 Working Women Education Fund.

Broder, John M. 2002. "Family Leave in California Includes Pay Benefit." *New York Times*, September 24.

Budig, Michelle, and Paula England. 2001. "The Wage Penalty for Motherhood." *American Sociological Review* 66: 204–25.

California Chamber of Commerce. 2004. *Managing Leaves of Absence in California Made Easy!* Sacramento: California Chamber of Commerce.

Calnen, Gerald. 2007. "Paid Maternity Leave and Its Impact on Breastfeeding in the United States: An Historic, Economic, Political, and Social Perspective." *Breastfeeding Medicine* 2 (1): 34–44.

Cobble, Dorothy Sue. 2004. *The Other Women's Movement: Workplace Justice and Social Rights in Modern America*. Princeton: Princeton University Press.

Correll, Shelley J., Stephen Benard, and In Paik. 2007. "Getting a Job: Is There a Motherhood Penalty?" *American Journal of Sociology* 112: 1297–1338.

Dark, Taylor E. 1999. *The Unions and the Democrats: An Enduring Alliance*. Ithaca: Cornell University Press.

DeParle, Jason. 2012. "Two Classes, Divided by 'I Do.'" *New York Times*, July 15, A1.

Dobbin, Frank. 2009. *Inventing Equal Opportunity*. Princeton: Princeton University Press.

Dorfman, Lori, and Elena O. Lingas. 2003. *Making the Case for Paid Family Leave: How California's Landmark Law Was Framed in the News*. Issue 14. Berkeley: Berkeley Media Studies Group. http://paidfamilyleave.org/pdf/dorfman.pdf.

Dube, Arindrajit, and Ethan Kaplan. 2002. "Paid Family Leave in California: An Analysis of Costs and Benefits." Unpublished manuscript, June 19. http://www.paidfamilyleave.org/pdf/dube.pdf.

Edds, Kimberly. 2002. "Calif. Adopts Family Leave: Law Mandates Paid Time Off." *Washington Post*, September 24, A3.

Esping-Andersen, Gosta. 1990. *The Three Worlds of Welfare Capitalism*. Princeton: Princeton University Press.

——. 2009. *The Incomplete Revolution: Adapting to Women's New Roles*. Malden, Mass.: Polity Press.

Fendel, Nina, Linda Gregory, Joannie Chang, and Netsy Firestein. 2003. "California's New Paid Family Leave Law: Family Temporary Disability Insurance (FTDI)." *California Public Employee Relations* 161 (August): 11–16.

Firestein, Netsy, and Nicola Dones. 2007. "Unions Fight for Work and Family Policies—Not for Women Only." In *The Sex of Class: Women Transforming American Labor*, edited by Dorothy Sue Cobble, 140–57. Ithaca: Cornell University Press.

Firestein, Netsy, Ann O'Leary, and Zoe Savitsky. 2011. *A Guide to Implementing Paid Family Leave: Lessons from California*. Berkeley: Labor Project for Working Families and Center on Health, Economic and Family Security (CHEFS). http://www.working-families.org/publications/pfl_guide.pdf

Fligstein, Neil, and Ofer Sharone. 2002. "Work in the Postindustrial Economy of California." In *The State of California Labor 2002* (University of California Institute for Labor and Employment), 67–93. Berkeley: University of California Press.

Folbre, Nancy, ed. 2012. *For Love and Money: Care Provision in the United States*. New York: Russell Sage Foundation.

Fraser, Nancy. 1994. "After the Family Wage: Gender Equality and the Welfare State." *Political Theory* 22: 591–618.

Freeman, Richard B. 2007. *America Works: Critical Thoughts on the Exceptional U.S. Labor Market*. New York: Russell Sage Foundation.

Galinsky, Ellen, Kerstin Aumann, and James T. Bond. 2011. *Times Are Changing: Gender and Generation at Work and at Home*. New York: Families and Work Institute. http://familiesandwork.org/site/research/reports/Times_Are_Changing.pdf.

Geissinger, Steve. 2002. "Davis Signs Paid Family Leave Law: Landmark Legislation Starts in 2004 and Is Hailed by Labor, Slammed by Business Groups." *Oakland Tribune*, September 24.

Gerson, Kathleen. 2010. *The Unfinished Revolution: How a New Generation Is Reshaping Family, Work and Gender in America*. New York: Oxford University Press.

Gerstel, Naomi, and Amy Armenia. 2009. "Giving and Taking Family Leaves: Right or Privilege?" *Yale Journal of Law and Feminism* 21 (1): 161–84.

Gerstel, Naomi, and Dan Clawson. 2001. "Unions' Responses to Family Concerns." *Social Problems* 48 (2): 277–97.

Girion, Lisa, and Megan Garvey. 2002. "Davis OKs Paid Family Leave Bill." *Los Angeles Times*, September 24, B1.

Glass, Jennifer. 2004. "Blessing or Curse? Work-Family Policies and Mothers' Wage Growth over Time." *Work and Occupations* 31: 367–94.

Gornick, Janet C., and Marcia K. Meyers. 2003. *Families That Work: Policies for Reconciling Parenthood and Employment*. New York: Russell Sage Foundation.

——, eds. 2009. *Gender Equality: Transforming Family Divisions of Labor*. Vol. 6 of *The Real Utopias Project*, edited by Erik Olin Wright. New York: Verso.

Guendelman, Sylvia, Jessica Lang Kosa, Michelle Pearl, Steve Graham, Julia Goodman, and Martin Kharrazi. 2009. "Juggling Work and Breastfeeding: Effects of Maternity Leave and Occupational Characteristics." *Pediatrics* 123 (1): 38–46.

Hays, Sharon. 1996. *The Cultural Contradictions of Motherhood*. New Haven: Yale University Press.

Heymann, Jody. 2000. *The Widening Gap: Why America's Working Families Are in Jeopardy and What Can Be Done about It*. New York: Basic Books.

Heymann, Jody, and Alison Earle. 2010. *Raising the Global Floor*. Stanford: Stanford University Press.

Hochschild, Arlie. 1997. *The Time Bind: When Work Becomes Home and Home Becomes Work*. New York: Metropolitan Books.

Human Rights Watch. 2011. *Failing Its Families: Lack of Paid Leave and Work-Family Supports in the US*. New York: Human Rights Watch. http://www.hrw.org/sites/default/files/reports/us0211webwcover.pdf.

Institute for Women's Policy Research. 2010. "Majority of Voters Support Workplace Flexibility, Job Quality and Family Support Policies." Press release, October 29. http://www.iwpr.org/press-room/press-releases/majority-of-workers-support-workplace-flexibility-job-quality-and-family-support-policies.

Jacobs, Jerry A., and Kathleen Gerson. 2004. *The Time Divide: Work, Family, and Gender Inequality*. Cambridge: Harvard University Press.

Jacoby, Sanford M. 1997. *Modern Manors: Welfare Capitalism since the New Deal*. Princeton: Princeton University Press.

Jones, Gregg. 2002. "Davis to Sign Bill Allowing Paid Family Leave." *Los Angeles Times*, September 23, A1.

Kaiser Family Foundation. 2003. *Women, Work, and Family Health: A Balancing Act*. Menlo Park, Calif.: Kaiser Family Foundation. http://www.kff.org/womenshealth/loader.cfm?url=/commonspot/security/getfile.cfm&PageID=14293.

Kantor, Jodi. 2006. "On the Job, Nursing Mothers Find a 2-Class System." *New York Times*, September 1, 1.

Kelly, Erin L. 2010. "Failure to Update: An Institutional Perspective on Noncompliance with the Family and Medical Leave Act." *Law and Society Review* 44 (1): 33–66.

Klein, Jennifer. 2003. *For All These Rights: Business, Labor and the Shaping of America's Public-Private Welfare State*. Princeton: Princeton University Press.

Koss, Natalie. 2003. "The California Temporary Disability Insurance Program." *Journal of Gender, Social Policy & the Law* 11 (2): 1079–88.

Kramer, Amit. 2008. "Unions as Facilitators of Employment Rights: An Analysis of Individuals' Awareness of Parental Leave in the National Longitudinal Survey of Youth." *Industrial Relations* 47 (4): 651–58.

Labor Project for Working Families. 2003. *Putting Families First: How California Won the Fight for Paid Family Leave*. http://paidfamilyleave.org/pdf/paidleavewon.pdf.

Lambert, Susan J. 2008. "Passing the Buck: Labor Flexibility Practices That Transfer Risk onto Hourly Workers." *Human Relations* 61: 1203–27.

Lareau, Annette. 2003. *Unequal Childhoods: Class, Race, and Family Life*. Berkeley: University of California Press.

Laughlin, Linda. 2011. *Maternity Leave and Employment Patterns of First-Time Mothers: 1961–2008*. Current Population Report P70–128. Washington, D.C.: U.S. Census Bureau. http://www.census.gov/prod/2011pubs/p70–128.pdf

Lester, Gillian. 2005. "A Defense of Paid Family Leave." *Harvard Journal of Law and Gender* 28 (1): 3–83.

Martin, Cathie Jo. 2000. *Stuck in Neutral: Business and the Politics of Human Capital Investment Policy*. Princeton: Princeton University Press.

Mason, Mary Ann, and Eve Mason Ekman. 2007. *Mothers on the Fast Track: How a New Generation Can Balance Family and Careers*. New York: Oxford University Press.

McCall, Leslie. 2001. *Complex Inequality: Gender, Race and Class in the New Economy*. New York: Routledge.

——. 2010. "What Does Class Inequality among Women Look Like? A Comparison with Men and Families, 1970 to 2000." In *Social Class: How Does It Work?* ed. Annette Lareau and Dalton Conley, 293–325. New York: Russell Sage Foundation.

Merrick, Pat. 1948. "California's Disability Insurance System." *Insurance Law Journal* 304 (May): 371–81.

Milkman, Ruth, and Eileen Appelbaum. 2004. "Paid Family Leave in California: New Research Findings." In *The State of California Labor 2004* (University of California Institute for Labor and Employment), 45–67. Berkeley: University of California Press.

Mitchell, Daniel. J. B. 2002. "Impeding Earl Warren: California's Health Insurance Plan That Wasn't and What Might Have Been." *Journal of Health Politics, Policy and Law* 27 (6): 947–76.

National Partnership for Women and Families. 2012. Election Eve/Night Omnibus November 2012, http://www.nationalpartnership.org/site/DocServer/Lake_Research_and_Tarrance_Group_Omnibus_Poll_Results_fo.pdf?docID=11581.

Ness, Debra. 2008. "Writing the Next Chapter of the Family and Medical Leave Act—Building on a Fifteen Year History of Support for Workers." Written testimony for the U.S. Congress, Committee on Health, Education, Labor and Pensions, February 13. http://www.nationalpartnership.org/site/DocServer/DebraNess_WrittenTestimony_2–13–08.pdf?docID=2941.

Osborn, Grant M. 1958. *Compulsory Temporary Disability Insurance in the United States*. Homewood, Ill.: Richard D. Irwin Inc. for the S.S. Huebner Foundation for Insurance Education, University of Pennsylvania.

Paul, Pamela. 2011. "Not One to Compromise." *New York Times*. December 11.

Payne, Melanie. 2002. "State Measure Would Expand Family Leave Law." *Sacramento Bee*, June 3.

Raley, Sara, Suzanne M. Bianchi, and Wendy Wang. 2012. "When Do Fathers Care? Mothers' Economic Contribution and Fathers' Involvement in Child Care. "*American Journal of Sociology* 117 (5): 1422–59.

Rossin-Slater, Maya, Christopher Ruhm, and Jane Waldfogel. 2013. "The Effects of California's Paid Family Leave Program on Mothers' Leave Taking and Subsequent Labor Market Outcomes." *Journal of Policy Analysis and Management* 32: 224–45.

Ruhm, Christopher J. 1997. "Policy Watch: The Family and Medical Leave Act." *Journal of Economic Perspectives* 11: 175–86.

———. 2000. "Parental Leave and Child Health." *Journal of Health Economics* 19: 931–60.

Saraceno, Chiara. 2004. "De-Familialization or Re-Familialization? Trends in Income-Tested Family Benefits." In *Solidarity between the Sexes and the Generations: Transformations in Europe*, ed. Trudie Knijn and Aafke Komter, 68–88. Northampton, Mass.: Edward Elgar Publishers.

Schuster, Mark A., Paul J. Chung, Marc N. Elliott, Craig F. Garfield, Katherine D. Vestal, and David J. Klein. 2008. "Awareness and Use of California's Paid Family Leave Insurance among Parents of Chronically Ill Children." *Journal of the American Medical Association* 300 (9): 1047–55.

———. 2009. "Perceived Effects of Leave from Work and the Role of Paid Leave among Parents of Children with Special Health Care Needs." *American Journal of Public Health* 99 (4): 698–705.

Sherriff, Rona. 2007. *Balancing Work and Family*. Sacramento: California Senate Office of Research.

Slaughter, Anne-Marie. 2012. "Why Women Still Can't Have It All." *Atlantic* 310 (1) (July–August): 84–102.

Somers, Margaret R., and Fred Block. 2005. "From Poverty to Perversity: Ideas, Markets, and Institutions over 200 Years of Welfare Debate." *American Sociological Review* 70: 260–87.

Statutes of California. Various years.

Stewart, Jack, Allan Zaremberg, and Bill Hauck. 2003. "An Ailing State? Business Climate Is Killing California's Economy." *San Diego Union-Tribune*, July 31.

Stone, Pamela. 2007. *Opting Out: Why Women Really Quit Careers and Head Home*. Berkeley: University of California Press.

Taylor, Zoe. 2002. "Chamber Backs 'No on SB1661' Coalition." *Ventura County Star*, August 25.

U.S. Department of Labor. 1952. *California Disability Insurance Program*. U.S. Bureau of Employment Security. Washington, D.C.: March 1952.

———. 2001. *Balancing the Needs of Families and Employers: Family and Medical Leave Surveys, 2000 Update*. Rockville, Md.: Westat.

———. 2011a. *Women in the Labor Force: A Databook*. U.S. Bureau of Labor Statistics Report 1034. http://www.bls.gov/cps/wlf-databook-2011.pdf.

———. 2011b. *National Compensation Survey: Employee Benefits in the United States, March 2011*. U.S. Bureau of Labor Statistics Bulletin 2771. http://www.bls.gov/ebs/benefits/2011/ebbl0048.pdf.

———. 2012a. "American Time Use Survey—2011 Results." News release USDL-12–1246. http://www.bls.gov/news.release/atus.nr0.htm/

———. 2012b. "Access to and Use of Leave: 2011 Data from the American Time Use Survey." News release USDL-12–1648. www.bls.gov/news.release/leave.nr0.htm.

Valian, Virginia. 1998. *Why So Slow? The Advancement of Women*. Cambridge: MIT Press.

Van Houtven, Courtney Harold, and Edward C. Norton. 2004. "Informal Care and Health Care Use of Older Adults." *Journal of Health Economics* 23 (6): 1159–80.

Vogel, Lise. 1993. *Mothers on the Job: Maternity Policy in the U.S. Workplace*. New Brunswick, N.J.: Rutgers University Press.

Waldfogel, Jane. 1997. "The Effect of Children on Women's Wages." *American Sociological Review* 62 (2): 209–17.

———. 1999. "Family Leave Coverage in the 1990s." *Monthly Labor Review* 122 (10): 13–21.

———. 2001. "Family and Medical Leave: Evidence from the 2000 Surveys." *Monthly Labor Review*, 124 (9): 17–23.

Warren, Elizabeth, and Amelia Warren Tyagi. 2003. *The Two-Income Trap*. New York: Basic Books.

White, Karen, Linda Houser, and Elizabeth Nisbet. 2013. *Policy in Action: New Jersey's Family Leave Program at Age Three*. New Brunswick, N.J.: Center for Women and Work, Rutgers University.

Williams, Joan. 2010. *Reshaping the Work-Family Debate: Why Men and Class Matter*. Cambridge: Harvard University Press.

Williams, Joan, and Heather Boushey. 2010. *The Three Faces of Work-Family Conflict: The Poor, the Professionals, and the Missing Middle*. San Francisco: Center for American Progress and Work Life Law, UC Hastings College of the Law.

Workplace Flexibility 2010 (Georgetown Law School) and the Berkeley Center on Health, Economic and Family Security (CHEFS) 2010. *Family Security Insurance: A New Foundation for Economic Security*. http://www.familysecurityinsurance.org/.

Index